AVA GARDNER

AVA GARDNER

An Illustrated History of the Movies

by
JUDITH M. KASS

General Editor: **TED SENNETT**

A HARVEST/HBJ BOOK

For my husband Milt

AVA GARDNER
An Illustrated History of the Movies

Copyright©1977 by Jove Publications Inc.

First Harvest/HBJ edition published August 1977

ISBN: 0-15-609425-8

Library of Congress Catalog Card Number: 77-76456

Printed in the United States of America

JOVE PUBLICATIONS, INC.
(Harcourt Brace Jovanovich)
757 Third Avenue, New York, N.Y. 10017

Library of Congress Cataloging in Publication Data

Kass, Judith M.
Ava Gardner

1. Gardner, Ava, 1922–   2. Moving-picture actors
    and actresses—United States—Biography
PN2287.G37K37   791.43' 028' 0924 (B)   77-76456
        ISBN 0-15-609425-8

Layout and Design by ANTHONY BASILE

ACKNOWLEDGMENTS

My sincere thanks to Bernard L. Glaser, Herman Kass and Ed Riester of Avco Embassy; John Cocchi; Doug Lemza of Films Incorporated; Mary Corliss, Jeff Schulman, Emily Sieger and Charles Silver of The Museum of Modern Art Film Department; Raymond Rohauer, Alice Geyer and Gene Giaquinto of Universal Pictures; and Lou Valentino—but especially to Joseph Balian and Barbara J. Humphrys of The Library of Congress Motion Picture Section.

Photographs: Jerry Vermilye, The Memory Shop,
Movie Star News, and the companies that produced
and distributed the films of Ava Gardner

CONTENTS

"Whatever it is, you name it. Whether you're born with it or catch it from a public drinking cup, Maria had it," said Edmond O'Brien of Ava Gardner in *The Barefoot Contessa*, and the "it" he referred to, whether in the possession of Clara Bow or Gardner, is an attribute so potent as to be virtually unmeasurable. This quality has ensured her an enduring appeal and a career which has outlasted those of her more obviously gifted contemporaries. The movie-going public, for the most part, delighted in her headline-making escapades which only seemed to increase her allure—a magnetism which soon became international. Gardner fought and swore in public, had her behind pinched in Rio de Janeiro, discarded husbands and boyfriends like used Kleenex—and the public's only response was to clamor for more films starring this sullen and enigmatic beauty.

Gardner got by for years with a minimal amount of acting talent and compensated for the deficiency with her particular brand of charismatic earthiness. The secret of Gardner's appeal is obvious. Men didn't want to share a soda and two straws with her the way they would have with Betty Grable; they wanted to share her bed. And the screen image Gardner projected was just as interested in the idea as the men were, but there

INTRODUCTION: THE LADY HAS GUTS

were some questions in the minds of her screen partners that had to be answered on the way to the boudoir. (These questions might have been answered had she worked with a director like Howard Hawks, who could have brought out her untapped resources as a comedienne.) They are: 1) was she a "good guy"?; 2) could she be trusted?; and 3) did she have staying power? The answers were as complex and multi-faceted as her roles. And these are no rhetorical questions posed by a series of cinematic lovers. They are central to any reading of Gardner's filmic character and to anything more than the most superficial comprehension of her personality.

Above all, the Gardner female wanted acceptance, for the most part on her own terms; yet she also wanted emphatic approval by the hero she sought. And how she sought! From Texas to Wiesbaden, from Kenya to Peking, Gardner met and challenged her men. She gave them her roughest side and if they could take it and came back for more, she folded. The iron-spined vixen simply melted, curling up like a kitten and mewing contentedly. Once tamed, the Gardner heroine was a docile, domesticated helpmate.

For if men's desires for Gardner were carnal, she had something quite different, and much more lasting, in mind. As she says, "That's the racket to be in—marriage and kids." "It's been everything." "You're the only man I could ever love." "I'm only trying to be happy." "It's as if we were under a spell." Gardner, the penthouse vampire, turned out to be a romantic *hausfrau*, happy to live for and through her men. The Gardner heels never clicked officiously through the halls of business, nor did she get herself up in the forbidding garb of the professional career woman. Retiring, self-abnegating, she was, however, frequently cursed in her search for the perfect mate. Finding herself stranded in Africa minus her maharajah (*Mogambo*), she turns to the first man she finds. She and Clark Gable have a fling, but when she sees he's in love with Grace Kelly, she backs away tactfully. Gardner knows he's "the man," so her hesitation at his final summons is a matter of pride rather than a pause for reflection. Gardner's commitments are total, which explains why her Julie LaVerne (*Show Boat*) slides quickly toward the gutter when her husband leaves her. No other life has any claim on her or meaning for her; she needs a man to feel complete, not because she is

spiritually empty or without intellectual resources, but because of a deep, inner need unrelated to sex. But Gardner is no passive receptacle for masculine ardor. She is an adventuress, foraging for her lover through the glittering capitals of the world, and through some stagnant backwaters, too. As early as 1946 (*Whistle Stop*) she turned up at a railroad crossing with an unexplained mink on her shoulders and thirty years later, she's still at it. In *The Cassandra Crossing*, she totes her gigolo around Europe like a pet dog. She is as active in her professional life as she is in her quest for the right man. Witness Maria Vargas' asking her director (in *The Barefoot Contessa*) if he can help her become an actress and not merely a star; her businesslike handling of communications at the *Bhowani Junction*; or, even in an incomparably poorer film, *Lone Star*, her insistence on knowing the truth, as an editor, about Gable's shady dealings as a purveyor of cattle to the government.

In many films Gardner appears to be a sleepwalker, moving through a reverie so private and personal she has to be jolted awake. Pandora (of *Pandora and the Flying Dutchman*) is such a woman and her narcissism is a reflection of Isabel Lorrison's (*East Side, West Side*) hardened solipsism, as is Maria Vargas with her haughty

As Lady Susan Ashlow in THE LITTLE HUT (1957)

As Eleanor Holbrook in
SEVEN DAYS IN MAY (1964)

longing and faraway stares.

Each is countered, however, by the confused but generous and other-directed personalities of women such as those she played in *Bhowani Junction* and *Show Boat*. For every entranced female like Maria Vargas or Venus (in *One Touch of Venus*) there is an earthy, raucous Maxine Faulk (*Night of the Iguana*) or a restive, unhappy Brett (*The Sun Also Rises*) who fails in her search for peace and fulfillment.

A corollary to Gardner's romantic suffering was a trait demonstrated early in her career—self-disgust—which evidences itself repeatedly throughout her films. "I'm poison to myself and everyone around me," she tells Edmond O'Brien in *The Killers*. Her Barbara Beaurevel, in *My Forbidden Past*, hates herself for trying to wreck Robert Mitchum's marriage, but plunges willfully ahead. The Julie of *Show Boat*'s last quarter despises the tramp she's become, but swallows her pride to inform Gaylord Ravenal of his wife's whereabouts. *The Barefoot Contessa* refers to her need for love as a disease: "When the sick one is yourself, you cannot run away." But the clearest evidence of Gardner's self-loathing is her remark to Gregory Peck in *On the Beach*: "I don't like myself much anyway."

Despite the misery these roles indicate, she managed to play parts with sufficient variety to show that she could have been a highly successful comedienne in the Carole Lombard/Jean Harlow manner, but MGM and her directors saw her physical attributes as more readily salable than her comedic gifts and concentrated, to the detriment of her career, on the "seductive goddess" aspect of her screen persona.

In spite of MGM's poor handling, she triumphed. No matter how dismal the vehicle, she usually got good reviews, and in 1953 she was number three in *Box Office Magazine*'s poll. Once free of the studio, she was able to choose roles which suited her image as the slightly tarnished woman-with-a-past. This conception is evidently one she feels most comfortable with, for, as she has aged, she has consistently appeared as the exotic, often wealthy, object of male ardor. From *55 Days at Peking* (1963) in which she played the mysterious Russian baroness, through the 1977 *Cassandra Crossing*, in which she depicts a married matron accompanied by her lover on their incessant travels around Europe, Gardner has been the rootless adventuress, refusing to accept her destiny. And this is the most attractive aspect of Gardner's personality, her absolute conviction that somewhere the right man exists, and that all she needs is the guts and persistence to find him.

"I was a strange little hillbilly."

Ava Lavinia Gardner was born on December 24, 1922 in Grabtown, a small crossroads community near Smithfield, North Carolina, in the heart of the tobacco-growing country. She was the youngest of Jonas Bailey and Mary Elizabeth Gardner's seven children. There were her eldest sister Beatrice, nicknamed "Bappie," Elsie Mae, Inez, Raymond (killed in a freak rifle accident when he was two years old), Melvin, and Myra. Inez remembers Ava's childhood: "I'm tired of reading about how Ava grew up in poverty working in the fields. We were poor, it's true, but wasn't everyone during the Depression? Actually, we had a fairly good life."

Jonas, a farmer, lost his property when Ava was two, and to help the family finances, Mary, who was nicknamed Molly, took a job cooking and cleaning at a teacher's dormitory in Smithfield. Ava accompanied her mother while her siblings remained with their father, who worked at a sawmill in Selma, a few miles away.

Later, in hopes that their fortunes would improve, the reunited family moved north to Newport News, Virginia where Molly ran a boarding house. They remained only two years before returning to Smithfield where, when Ava was sixteen years old, her father died. Later, she told a reporter, "When Daddy died, I had a guilty feeling that I hadn't done all the things I should have to make his last days more pleasant."

The Gardners had always been poor and they were forced to send Ava to Smithfield High School in the same worn out clothes day after day. Remembering these awkward teenage years, Ava remarked, "I was a strange little hillbilly. What a generation! No wonder we were all neurotic and crazy."

She was also a beautiful, leggy brunette, continually sought after for dates. But her mother discouraged her would-be boyfriends and Ava herself was painfully shy. She recalls saying goodnight on her porch to a boyfriend and letting the boy embrace her. Molly pounced on them and ordered the boy away so forcefully that Ava burst into tears. She was embarrassed enough to try to wash off the "dirt I was sure I had contacted from that kiss." A further social barrier was her thick Tarheel accent. When she introduced herself as "Avah Gadnuh," she could be assured of hoots of derisive laughter.

After graduation, Ava attended Atlantic Christian College in Wilson, North Carolina where she studied to be a secretary and lived with her mother at the teacherage in

16

As an MGM starlet

Rock Ridge, near Wilson. "I never had any ambitions to be anything but dead in those days," Ava said later. "I didn't have any interests, and there is nothing I wanted to do. If I hadn't gone to Hollywood, I suppose I would have become a secretary."

In the early summer of 1941, Ava went to New York to visit her sister Bappie, who had married a photographer, Larry Tarr. Tarr saw immediately that his sister-in-law had possibilities and, needing a fresh model to photograph for the Fifth Avenue shop where he worked, Tarr took hundreds of pictures of Ava, some of which wound up in the display window. Barney Duhan, an errand clerk in the legal department of Metro-Goldwyn-Mayer, spotted them on his way to a party. Duhan remembers seeing those photos: "It was the face of the kind of girl you want to marry. It was vibrant!" He called the shop, pretending to be a talent scout from MGM, and said he wanted to meet the girl whose picture was in the window. Ava had already returned to North Carolina, but, believing Duhan's story, Bappie offered to send for her right away. Duhan requested that the Tarrs send him some pictures, which he showed to Marvin Schenck, the man in charge of talent. Schenck was impressed, as was Howard Deitz, the head of publicity. Ava came back to New

York and, accompanied by Bappie, presented herself to Schenck for an interview and a screen test.

At MGM, representative Ben Jacobson gave her a script to read, whereupon Ava's Tarheel accent emerged, making everything she said virtually unintelligible. She was "Avah Gadnuh" again. Jacobson decided to make a silent test and he and Schenck decreed that Ava should have the most glamorous lighting possible. Al Altman, who directed the test, said that "she was hopeless." But publicist Silas Seadler recollects, "She just took our collective breaths away. Clumsy she may have been, talk she could not. But what a dame!" The Hollywood studio concurred and one MGM official exclaimed, "She can't act; she didn't talk; she's sensational. Get her out here."

So out "here" she went. Bappie, who had divorced Tarr, chaperoned Ava to California and lived with her in a succession of unprepossessing apartments. Bappie has remained devoted to her sister throughout the latter's career, helping Ava set up several households in the United States and Europe. A friendly, light-haired woman, Bappie has been content to be her famous sibling's friend, and although she has a life of her own, often drops everything to hurry to Ava's side when she's needed.

Ava was paid $50 a week with

options and started on a regimen of acting, diction and make-up lessons. She was, in every sense of the word, a "manufactured" star, as had been Lana Turner before her and Kim Novak afterward. The studio simply took over and surrounded her with those whose talents could help her overcome her deficiencies. During this period, Lillian Burns, MGM's small, fiery acting teacher, was the most influential person in Ava's life. As an actress—her only assets were her sexual magnetism, her natural beauty, and an attractive laugh —Ava Gardner, the potential star, had to be created from the bottom up.

Ava recalls her first days at MGM: "They sent me to the hairdresser, and he told me to take the gum out of my mouth. I was never so ashamed in my life." She also spent hours with publicist Ann Straus posing for cheesecake and publicity stills. "I don't remember how many swimsuits I wore out —without getting near the water," Ava complained later. Her lessons and the endless photographic sessions were as close to the movie business as she got. She had yet to face a motion picture camera after months on the lot. "It never dawned on me that I wasn't going to be a smash right away," she said when she discovered how little progress she was making. Although she derided the glamour treatment she was getting, the eternal periods of being homogenized in MGM's make-up department until she looked like every other starlet, and despaired of ever making her acting debut, Ava was already exhibiting the contradictory strains of contempt and ambition which have marked her attitude to her work throughout her career. Ann Straus recalls: "Her indifference was a pose. Her drive was extraordinary and ruthless. She was determined to put up with all the nonsense to become a star."

In the midst of this early training period, Gardner met Mickey Rooney while he was shooting *Babes on Broadway*. Rooney was a confirmed lady killer and he was determined to have her. He remembers Gardner as having "black hair, an animal litheness, a face that bespoke both reserve and passion." At first, she was only minimally interested in Rooney, but he began a calculated barrage of gifts, notes and phone calls to which Gardner responded with an amused aloofness. Eventually, Rooney wore her down and they began to date. Louis B. Mayer, the studio chief, was furious, not wanting his biggest star, in whom millions of dollars were invested, to marry an obscure contract actress.

The youngsters (Rooney was twenty-one, Gardner nineteen) were wed more in an act of defiance in the face of general disapproval than because they felt any lasting affinity for one another. They were married, at the studio's insistence, in a small ceremony in Ballard, California on January 10, 1942. Rooney's mother granted the couple her official blessing: "I give the marriage three weeks before it's over."

But Gardner had a more pressing problem. Les Peterson, an MGM press agent, came along on their honeymoon by the sea at Monterey. "When you came down

THE FORTIES: STARTING OUT

"We were a couple of kids. We didn't have a chance."

to breakfast, he was there. When you had your dinner, he was there. When you went to bed, he damn near was there."

The marriage was in dire straits as soon as it had begun, with Rooney, the life of every party, cavorting till the wee hours with his cronies, or playing golf while Gardner stayed at home alone, her home-cooked meals spoiling as she waited for her bridegroom. Gardner explained the difficulties their immaturity caused them: "We had no idea that marriage involved a meeting of minds. That it involved sharing of problems, planning together, making a life together." Their union lasted sixteen months and they were divorced without rancor. Gardner's comment on the break-up typifies the situation of many young stars who found themselves in similar circumstances: "We were a couple of kids. We didn't have a chance."

But Rooney did help the novice actress professionally. When she finally got out of her bathing suit and on to the set of *We Were Dancing* (1942) for her first walk-on, "Mickey showed me how to walk,

KID GLOVE KILLER (1942). With Marsha Hunt
and Lee Bowman

how to stand, what to do with my hands, how to ignore the camera." As Gardner was the first to admit, "If I ever do anything big, I'll owe it to Mickey."

After this inauspicious debut in a trite Norma Shearer vehicle, Gardner had another unbilled bit in the patriotic *Joe Smith, American* (1942); she was seen at ringside in *Sunday Punch* (1942); and she could be glimpsed in a car in *This Time for Keeps* (1942). Gardner appeared even more briefly as a movie cashier in an Our Gang short, *Mighty Lak a Goat* (1942) and she had another bit in *Calling Dr. Gillespie* (1942), part of the long-running series. She was a car hop in *Kid Glove Killer* (1942), a

department store salesgirl in *Reunion in France* (1942), and played another bit in *Pilot No. 5* (1943). Gardner, on loanout to Monogram, had billing and a real part in the innocuous East Side Kids caper, *Ghosts on the Loose* (1943). As Mary, she's kidnapped by a gang of Nazi saboteurs headed by Bela Lugosi and rescued by the Kids who land like the Marines on the baddies.

Hitler's Madman (1943) tells the true story of the Czech village of Lidice, which was destroyed by the Nazis in World War II, and the Czech assassination of Commander Heydrich. Gardner was a villager terrorized by the Germans. She was a hat check girl in *Lost*

23

GHOSTS ON THE LOOSE (1943). With Rick Vallin

MAISIE GOES TO RENO (1944). With Paul Cavanagh,
Ann Sothern, Marta Linden, and Donald Meek

SHE WENT TO THE RACES (1945). With James Craig and Frank Orth

Angel (1943), a Margaret O'Brien movie, and a receptionist in *Swing Fever* (1944). She played Jean Brown in another Dr. Gillespie film, *Three Men in White* (1944). As a seductive, presumed lush she was used by Lionel Barrymore as a vamp to see if Van Johnson had the will-power to resist her in favor of medicine. *The New York Times* said that "Ava Gardner turns in a sympathetic if not altogether convincing job as a lady who can suffer and have a firm chin."

Gardner had another bit in *Blonde Fever* (1944) and a larger part in one of the Ann Sothern series, *Maisie Goes to Reno* (1944). In the latter she plays Gloria Fullerton, a rich miss having her troubles with her penniless soldier husband, Tom Drake. Maisie patches up the young couple's difficulties and dispatches a gang of forgers into the bargain.

Gardner had two sequences in *Two Girls and a Sailor* (1944) as a showgirl who dances with servicemen at a club organized by June Allyson and Gloria DeHaven. Persuaded by her partner that she's tired and can nap while dancing, she nestles her head on his shoulder, then sleeps standing up. Another shot shows him passed out on *her* chest. Gardner also appears as a model in a dream sequence involving Allyson's romance with Van Johnson. The Gardner of this period stands erect as befits a

WHISTLE STOP (1946). With Tom Conway

graduate of MGM's glamour mill, has a pompadour, and a long forties hairdo and a sweet smile. Little more was required.

Gardner had third billing in *She Went to the Races* (1945), in which she played Hilda Spotts, a wealthy horse owner who gets involved in a complicated scheme hatched by four scientists to raise $20,000 for research by betting on the ponies. The object of her affection is James Craig whom she calls "Honeykins" and whom she loses in a bet to Frances Gifford. It was harmless fluff directed with a notable lack of verve by Willis Goldbeck.

Philip Yordan, the scenarist, remembers the struggle he and producer Seymour Nebenzal had to get *Whistle Stop* (1946) on the screen. They were stuck with George Raft and were looking for a leading lady. "We couldn't find anybody suitable, which is a polite way of saying no one wanted to play the part." They settled on Gardner, noting later, "Five thousand to Metro, and the dame was ours." But once on the set, Gardner's professional insecurity and inexperience emerged. According to Yordan, "She was just a sweet, confused girl trying very hard not to be a hick and failing." Yordan had to rewrite some scenes so that Gardner and Raft could manage the lines, thus vitiating the dramatic points he was trying to make.

The film United Artists finally

WHISTLE STOP (1946). With George Raft

With bridegroom Artie Shaw and Shaw's mother in 1945

released is a complicated melodrama involving Raft as a loafer and drunk loved inexplicably by Gardner, a possibly tarnished young lady who returns from two years in Chicago with a mink coat and a yen for still more of life's finer commodities. Raft, attempting to provide them, concocts a scheme to rob Tom Conway, a local shady character, which fails when Gardner gets in Raft's way. She subsequently persuades him to find an honest job.

Raft, stolid and fifty, and hardly the kind of man a twenty-three-year-old Gardner is likely to salute with "Hi ya, handsome," is a blank space on the screen. He fills it only with a frown and the sinister, all-knowing grin of a barracuda in gangster's clothing. Gardner is all posture and wardrobe. She stands like a ramrod, yielding only when she rails at Victor McLaglen, Raft's friend, for being a coward. The rain pouring over her in this scene seems to melt some of the starch from her body; she's more pliant and gives what appears to be a performance, though it's hard to tell from the third-rate movie Yordan ultimately culled from Maritta Wolff's trashy, pretentious novel. Leonide Moguy directs Gardner to capitalize on her physical appeal and seems to have had some notion of making a *film noir*. *Whistle Stop* is merely dark.

After her divorce, Gardner dated

28

string of eligible young men, including Howard Duff, Howard Hughes, and her ex-husband, for whom she still had a soft spot. Gardner explained her relationship with the reclusive Hughes: "He makes it easy for me when I want things easy. If you want to be quiet and left alone, he arranges it. He's just the ticket for a girl like me, from the Deep South and lazy."

While working with Van Heflin in *Kid Glove Killer*, Gardner met Heflin's wife, the quiet and sympathetic Frances, who became, after Bappie, Gardner's closest companion. It was Frances who introduced Gardner to Artie Shaw one night at the Mocambo. In addition to being an enormously talented clarinetist,

Shaw was an intelligent, self-educated man. He became immediately infatuated with Gardner and sought to bring her up to his intellectual level. He began by working on her feelings of insecurity, her conviction that she was only a piece of MGM's merchandise, a star without star ability.

At one time Gardner had said, "If I could be born over again, I'd want an education. When I left school, I discovered I was a dumbbell." Now she had a chance to act on her wish. She began seeing Shaw's analyst and, after she and Shaw were married—in October of 1945—she attended courses in economics and English literature at UCLA. Gardner's ambivalence

THE KILLERS (1946). With Burt Lancaster

THE KILLERS (1946). With Jeff Corey, Burt Lancaster, and Albert Dekker

about marriage and the conflicting demands of their careers brought the relationship to an end exactly one year later. In spite of the termination, Gardner, while achieving some perspective on their union, retained a certain regard for her former husband. Subsequently, she remarked, "How could I say anything against him when I learned about just plain thinking from him? Of my three husbands, I had the most admiration for Artie. I think he's impossible to live with or even to be friendly with but he is still a worthwhile human being.

"He taught me to study and I read a lot of books. Thanks to Artie, I read Ernest Hemingway's *Death in the Afternoon*, which meant I had a little to talk about with Hemingway. And it also introduced me to bullfighting. As a by-product of my marriage to Shaw, I own an extensive library of symphonic recordings."

MGM next loaned Gardner to Universal for *The Killers* (1946). The screen version of Ernest Hemingway's work retains only Nick Adams, a character from the author's short stories, and the device of the man who knows he's going to die and waits impassively for the end. The plot unfolds through a series of interconnecting flashbacks as several people tell their stories to Edmond O'Brien, an insurance investigator piecing together the convoluted events sur-

THE HUCKSTERS (1947).
With Clark Gable

THE HUCKSTERS (1947). With Clark Gable, Deborah Kerr, Gloria Holden, and Adolphe Menjou

rounding a robbery.

Gardner has a small but decisive role as Kitty Collins, the fatal woman whose treachery creates in Burt Lancaster, her inamorata, the ennui and acceptance of doom with which he faces his killers. Lancaster (in an effective screen debut) first sees Gardner leaning against a piano in a slinky, black satin dress and murmuring, "The More I Know of Love" (in her own husky voice). He's instantly smitten, a fall guy ready-made to take the rap when she's caught with some stolen jewelry. They're reunited when her current flame, Albert Dekker, is planning to rob a hat factory. Sultry and sensual, Gardner lounges on the bed like a cat in

heat, listening to the men's plans and waiting for something to galvanize her. Respite is not long in coming. Gardner and Lancaster make off with the profits from the heist, then Gardner two-times him, disappearing with the money.

Past and present converge at the end when O'Brien has unraveled the mystery and Dekker and Gardner, man and wife, are unmasked as the architects of Lancaster's demise. "I'm poison to myself and everyone around me," Gardner confesses to O'Brien and proceeds to prove it by urging her dying husband to declare her innocent and exonerate her of any blame arising from the mayhem they've caused together. Her hair falling over her face, she pleads, "Tell them I didn't know anything. Save me!" Gardner is the epitome of feminine deceit in the guise of persuasive candor.

Gardner and the entire cast are greatly abetted by Robert Siodmak's *film noir* directorial style and cameraman Norbert Brodine's lighting with its rich, contrasting blacks and whites, its shadows falling across the half-seen actions of corrupt men, and the film's general air of casual immorality.

During her career, Gardner has been criticized for having a thin, nasal voice. In fact, her voice is low and seductive, an attractive instrument which she uses, along with some eloquently erotic looks, to convince her men she loves them, or, as here, that she's on the up and up. Kitty Collins is one of the roles that shaped Gardner's image as a femme fatale, the sort of part she would regret in succeeding years. At the time, however, she was grateful for it. When producer Mark Hellinger decided to cast Gardner as *The Killers'* gun moll, she took her role seriously enough to have the films of several important actresses run off so she could study their facial expressions and mannerisms. "It paid off," she said. "For the first time in my life I got some good notices."

Back at her home studio, Gardner had another small role in *The Hucksters* (1947), which purports

SINGAPORE (1947). With Fred MacMurray

SINGAPORE (1947). As Linda

to be a behind-the-scenes look at the sycophants and neurotics who run the nation's advertising business. The film is elegant, gilded trash, promising more than it delivers and faking its profundity through the speeches of its stereotyped characters: Sydney Greenstreet as the crass, bullying manufacturer of Beautee Soap; Deborah Kerr as the high-minded war widow pursued by Clark Gable, the incorruptible advertising man who has Adolphe Menjou for his ulcer-ridden, toadying boss.

Gardner plays Jean Ogilvie, a nightclub singer and former girl friend of Gable's, a girl who's perfectly willing to catch him on the rebound if he can convince her he really cares for her. Gardner warbles a love song, "Don't Tell Me," in an appropriately torchy style and looks sultry, but unfortunately her voice is dubbed. Exclaiming over Kerr's family, Gardner utters a line which could come from her own biography: "That's the racket to be in—marriage and kids." But so alluring was the image of Gardner as a playgirl, whether naughty or nice, that her film characterizations followed her life story—she was often married but never a mother until late in her career, and then only on screen. In fact, one scene in *The Hucksters* shows her dolled up in a gingham apron, putting the finishing touches on a home-cooked meal for Gable, which misfires when she realizes he's in love with Kerr.

Although her part is small, Gardner brings warmth and humor to it as the kind of understanding, good-for-a-laugh girl every man wants somewhere in his life—at least once. But *The Hucksters* is all gloss and no substance—a message film with nothing to say.

Jean Ogilvie was, with Kitty Collins, the role that made Gardner a star. From then on, her name appeared above the title, although she made a great point of having strong co-stars so that she never had to carry a film by herself at the box office. Gardner insisted, for example, that Tyrone Power be cast as Jake Barnes in *The Sun Also Rises* so there would be a powerful name with hers and receipts would not be dependent on her presence alone.

Although she had become a star, as much through the efforts of others as through her own perseverance, Gardner's emerging status was not reflected in the caliber of the roles she played once she'd arrived at that elevated plateau. MGM lent her again to Universal for her next two films, which were so inferior that she resolved to take a hand in changing things. She declared, "After all, I'm not a kid anymore. When I first came out here I was lazy and dreamy. I wasn't interested in a career. Once

ONE TOUCH OF VENUS (1948). With Robert Walker

ONE TOUCH OF VENUS (1948). With Robert Walker

THE GREAT SINNER (1949). With Gregory Peck and Ethel Barrymore

my second marriage blew up, however, I realized that I'd better learn how to make a living. Now I'm ready to concentrate on my career."

In *Singapore* (1947) Gardner plays Linda Grahame, the girl soldier-of-fortune Fred MacMurray loves and almost marries on the eve of World War II. An air raid separates them; he believes she's dead and returns five years later to collect some pearls he smuggled and hid in the ceiling fan of his old hotel room. He also discovers that, in his absence, Gardner has lost her memory and married Roland Culver, a local businessman. A customs official, Richard Haydn, is convinced that MacMurray has the

pearls, which Thomas Gomez, a corrupt local, also covets. Inferring that Gardner knows their whereabouts, Gomez kidnaps her and tries to make her talk. In an attempt to rescue her, Gardner gets a bump on the head which restores her memory. MacMurray turns the pearls over to Haydn and prepares to leave Singapore, at which point Culver releases Gardner from her marriage vows and arranges to reunite her with MacMurray.

All this nonsense could have been mildly diverting fun if it had been handled tongue-in-cheek as a sleazy "B" film. But the cheap, backlot sets look merely tacky and never manage to convey the lure or mystery of the East. *Singapore* might have been shot in Hoboken. The script meanders from throbbing romance to Japanese bomb attacks to unspecified menace, with the characters looking confused, sinister or smug by turns. MacMurray clenches his jaw and does what he can with the unmalleable material, but Gardner is defeated by the lack of motivation and focus in her role. She slithers through the awkward theatrics looking even more dazed than most women who have lost their memories.

In *One Touch of Venus* (1948), derived from the Kurt Weill-Ogden Nash-S.J. Perelman stage musical, Gardner played a statue of the Anatolian Venus brought to life by a kiss from an impulsive window dresser, Robert Walker. The statue, scheduled for unveiling by department store owner Tom Conway, turns up missing from its pedestal and trails Walker around, causing him no end of embarrassment with his landlady, his job and his girl, Olga San Juan. The latter consoles herself with Walker's roommate, Dick Haymes, who helps a dubbed Ava sing "Speak Low," one of the two songs retained from the original Kurt Weill score; a new and much less felicitous tune, "My Heart is Showing," with lyrics by Ann Ronnell, has been added. Conway installs Gardner in the store's model home and starts making passes, while his girl Friday (Eve Arden in typical

THE GREAT SINNER (1949). With Walter Huston, Melvyn Douglas, and Gregory Peck

EAST SIDE, WEST SIDE (1949). With James Mason

acerbic form, but with less to work with than usual) snorts to cover her affection for her boss. At the finale, Gardner has gotten the right couples together and, the gods having recalled her to Mount Olympus, resumes her place on the pedestal. As Walker is mooning at her feet, a new salesgirl asks directions to the model home. It's Gardner as "Venus Jones." As they move off together, she remarks coyly, "Nobody's ever likely to meet two girls named Venus."

Walker plays the window trimmer as a frenzied, unsophisticated klutz, naive, boyish and not particularly romantic. Gardner is seductive and playful, falling in love with Walker because he's the first man

she sees. She has little to do but look gorgeous and pose in several attractive outfits which display her spectacular figure to its best advantage. It's as though everything she had learned about acting when playing Kitty Collins had been ignored. Given nothing to do, she creates a vacuum on screen. William A. Seiter's direction is heavy-handed and graceless, failing to extract even the modicum of humor remaining from the original play, which was artlessly adapted by Harry Kurnitz and Frank Tashlin.

In June of 1949, Gardner made one of her infrequent radio appearances. She acted on the CBS Prudential Family Hour in a program entitled "Exit Linda Davis." To

EAST SIDE, WEST SIDE (1949). With James Mason

THE BRIBE (1949). With John Hodiak and Robert Taylor

date, she has eschewed all television shows, at first because her MGM contract wouldn't permit it, and later because she simply couldn't be bothered.

Nowhere in MGM's *The Great Sinner* (1949) is it mentioned that Christopher Isherwood and Ladislas Fodor culled their story from Fyodor Dostoievsky's *The Gambler*, but a title announces that "The story is inspired by the work of a writer, a gambler himself, who played for his life and won immortality," and this principal character, played by Gregory Peck, is called Fedja. Dostoievsky *was* a great writer and a compulsive gambler, and to compound the many "coincidences," Agnes Moorehead plays a vicious old crone of a pawnbroker whom Peck contemplates murdering for her money (à la *Crime and Punishment*). Peck suffers dizzy spells—Dostoievsky was an epileptic; in 1863 he had an affair with Polina Suslova (she became Paulina in *The Gambler*), and traveled with her in Western Europe, another circumstance alluded to in the scenario. Although they are many, the coincidences end here, for whatever style *The Great Sinner* has derives not from Fodor and Isherwood's typewriters, nor their relationship to Dostoievsky's pen, but from the direction of Robert Siodmak and the photography of George Folsey. Siodmak and Folsey have contrived to light many

THE BRIBE (1949). With Robert Taylor

scenes ingeniously and to photograph them so picturesquely as to disguise the fact that this is strictly a backlot MGM production.

Peck meets Gardner (here playing one Pauline Ostrovsky) in Wiesbaden where *she* is the obsessive gambler and he the detached and ironically amused writer seeking material for his next book. They fall in love, and she renounces the life of the casino while he succumbs to gambling fever, winning enough to release her from a debt she and her father (Walter Huston) owe to casino proprietor Melvyn Douglas. He then loses this and more, sinking deeper into debt until he's lost his self-respect and his hotel room, winding up in the servants' quarters whence Gardner arrives to rescue him. During this time, Peck has managed to pen a little something he calls *The Confession of a Sinner*, which Gardner reads while waiting for him to recover from an illness so she can whisk him away and, presumably, reform *him*. "This isn't the last chapter," she croons, nestling him to her shoulder.

The story is told in a flashback with Peck narrating the on-screen events. As the narrator, he isn't able to make Isherwood's and Fodor's self-consciously literary speeches convincing, and as an actor, he's carved in granite; the light of a great desire—for the roulette tables—glimmers only faintly in his eyes. Gardner is sumptuously gowned and manages to suggest the aura of a scarlet woman whose vice is games of chance and, only secondarily, men. But forced to speak lines like "My first grand passion was the jack of spades," and behave like a superstitious, if gorgeous, witch, Gardner has no better luck in *The Great Sinner* than Peck. When she appears at his bedside, stripped of her finery and simply made up, she is truly, in appearance at least, the redeemed lover, and she looks all of nineteen years old.

East Side, West Side (1949) pits the allure of the West Side flat, a luxurious one off Washington Square, and its occupant, Gardner (as Isabel Lorrison) against the East Side duplex James Mason inhabits with his long-suffering wife, Barbara Stanwyck. Gardner, whose favors Mason has enjoyed previously, strolls back into his life, makes him miserable, taunts Stanwyck with her husband's infidelities, and finishes the film dead on her own foot-deep pile carpet, the victim of still another predatory female. Stanwyck refuses to forgive Mason again and finds solace with Van Heflin.

Isobel Lennart's screenplay conforms to the Marcia Davenport novel, and she has preserved the book's aura of trashy elegance, overall silliness and its pseudo-profound talk. Mervyn LeRoy directed with an eye for the decor—he does very little to help the actors wade through the banalities Lennart has retained in this overlong adaptation. Mason, attempting a mid-Atlantic style of diction, sounds garbled, Stanwyck is iron-jawed and Heflin friendly. Gardner comes off very well against these veterans; she is persuasively rotten, selfish and seductive with Mason, but tenaciously smug when telling Stanwyck, in their one scene together, that Mason will come running whenever she calls. *Variety* reported that "... Miss Gardner probably grabs off top honors as the willful and attractive vixen," but Bosley Crowther, who as long as he reviewed Gardner's films— from 1946 to 1967—never had a kind word for her work, no matter what the vehicle (a peculiar and unexplained animus), said that "Ava Gardner plays the charmer like a hash-slinger, which she claims to be."

Interestingly, Cyd Charisse has a medium-sized role as a good girl who helps Mason, and is, coincidentally, a friend of Heflin's. Charisse, even when co-starred with Gene Kelly and Fred Astaire, seemed, with her strong facial and physical resemblance to Gardner, to be filling roles Gardner might have had if she had been, like Audrey Hepburn, more versatile.

The Bribe (1949) is one of those intrigue movies where the hero has only one name, the dialogue is mostly cheap gangster patter and everyone perspires heavily except the heroine (Gardner as Elizabeth Hintten), who looks as cool as the proverbial cucumber. Marguerite Roberts fashioned a cryptic film from Frederick Nebel's story and Robert Z. Leonard directed it with a certain steamy ambiance, strongly reminiscent of that provided for *To Have and Have Not* five years earlier. He is helped immeasurably by cinematographer Joseph Ruttenberg's shadow-filled low-key lighting. Taylor speaks a voice-over narration which detracts from one's comprehension of the plot rather more than it adds. He behaves with cynical integrity as a Federal agent sent to the town of Carlotta on a Central American island to investigate the smuggling of surplus airplane engines into South America by, among others, John Hodiak.

Gardner plays Hodiak's loyal, unsuspecting wife, who sings in a cantina and falls in love with Taylor. Her song, "Situation Wanted," is dubbed, but the voice is closer to Gardner's speaking voice than the one substituted for hers in *The Hucksters*. She's a convincingly slinky chanteuse, gliding around the club floor in black sequins, her wedding ring purposely

left in her dressing room so that the male patrons will think she's available and throw more money. Otherwise she looks worried or amorous, and pads around Carlotta in huaraches and peasant blouses as befits a lady stranded in the tropics.

The bribe of the title is offered to Taylor by Charles Laughton to forget what he's learned. Laughton, who plays—in Taylor's words—"a pie-shaped, small-time drifter," does one of the "schtiks" he usually enjoys: rubbing his bad feet, showing Taylor the x-rays from his podiatrist, and complaining that he needs his cut of the profits for a foot operation. His performance is the one pleasure the film provides, and Taylor justifiably felt that *The Bribe* was the low point of his career. Hodiak conveniently suffers a heart attack, which paves the way for Gardner to end the film in Taylor's arms. As Taylor tries to revive the dying man, Laughton tells him, "T'ain't no use," but he might have been talking about the movie.

In Gardner's companionship, Taylor found some compensation for making this film. He was having a hard time in his marriage to Barbara Stanwyck (coincidentally Gardner's love rival that same year in *East Side, West Side*). They were divorced three years later. Taylor and Gardner met occasionally, sometimes at his mother's house, a fact which caused this religious woman much grief.

Gardner was about to enter the era of her greatest stardom, with three films revolving around her beauty and presence (*Pandora and the Flying Dutchman*, *The Barefoot Contessa* and *Bhowani Junction*) and a part written for her in a fourth film (Cynthia in *The Snows of Kilimanjaro*). Nevertheless she still had grave doubts about being an actress. As she said, "I never wanted to be a star. Not now. Not the day I took a screen test."

But this remark was the product of her habitual ambivalence. In the next thirteen years she would receive her only Academy Award nomination (for *Mogambo*), make the most money of her career and, finally, leave MGM. Along the way there were more stumbling blocks to negotiate, among them, the studio's notion that her popularity was strong enough to survive the many mediocre films she was assigned. Typically, Gardner did better on loan-out, but even that was an uncertain proposition.

Ava Gardner met Frank Sinatra when both were filming at MGM, and she had professed nothing but hostility for his egotistical manner until they encountered each other at a New York premiere in 1950, and then met shortly thereafter in Palm Springs. At that time Sinatra had already separated from Nancy, his wife of many years, so Gardner was justifiably bitter when she was crucified in print as a home wrecker. Since the couple hardly made a secret of their fights, or their affair, which lasted for two years, the press was able to follow their activities with its customary rapacity.

Gardner and Sinatra were finally married on November 7, 1951 at the Philadelphia home of Lester Sacks, a friend of Sinatra. Looking out of the window, Sinatra found members of the fourth estate avidly waiting for a glimpse of the couple. "How did these creeps know we were here?" he snarled. Then, recovering his charm, Sinatra and his bride posed for the official photographer, kissing and cutting their wedding cake as he cooed, "Well, we finally made it."

As they battled their way through their courtship, so they continued during their married life. (In anger, Gardner tossed her engagement ring out the window of her room at New York's Hampshire House hotel. It was never recovered.) Gardner married Sinatra

THE FIFTIES: THE TOP

"I was much better equipped for having babies."

when his career was at low ebb. Before she left to film *Mogambo* (1953) in Africa, Gardner pleaded personally with Harry Cohn, the head of Columbia Pictures, to give Sinatra the part of Maggio in *From Here to Eternity*, a role he had long coveted. Sinatra accompanied her to Africa, then flew back from Nairobi to test for the role. The Academy Award he won for Maggio gave Sinatra the boost he needed to put him on top again. As Gardner said later, "Frank Sinatra was supposed to be all through when I married him. I didn't believe it—and I didn't steal him from Nancy. I stood beside him when things were the roughest. Then he got big again and became his old arrogant self."

Although she frequently expressed her preference for a home and family over a career, by all accounts Gardner was as ambivalent on this subject as she was about her profession. When her marriage to Mickey Rooney was over, she claimed that he didn't want a child, but Rooney reported in his autobiography: "Pregnancy terrified Ava. I don't know why. I don't think Ava knew why. I only know

With husband Frank Sinatra in 1951

With Frank Sinatra in 1952

that when Ava was nineteen, the thought of having a baby filled her with a nameless, unreasoning dread."

During her marriage to Artie Shaw, the couple was at such emotional and intellectual odds that it is unlikely that Gardner wanted a child by him. She talked about leaving the movie business at this time. It is apparent that she was terrified by her successes in *Whistle Stop* and *The Killers*, and was having second thoughts about being a star. For a time, Gardner even kept the inexpensive coat she came to Hollywood in as a reminder that she shouldn't be overimpressed with her newfound stardom.

Gardner's attitude changed while she was married to Frank Sinatra. She was pregnant while shooting *Mogambo* in Africa, and reports have varied over the years as to whether, when she became ill and flew to a London hospital, she had a miscarriage or an abortion. Although she later told Joe Hyams, "All of my life I had wanted a baby and the news that I lost [it] was the cruelest blow I had ever received."[*] Robert Surtees, the film's cinematographer, remembers the events differently: "Ava hated Frank so intensely by this stage, she couldn't stand the idea of having his baby. She went to London to have

an abortion. I know because my wife went to London to be at her side at all times. . . ."

Just before her last estrangement from Sinatra, Gardner was still insisting that she wanted his child: "The one thing I want more than anything else in the world, I don't have. I want a child. We want one. That's the only thing in the world that really counts." But by 1961 she had become more realistic about herself and her life style. As she told Rona Jaffe: "If I had a baby, two years later I would be bored with it and forget all about it—so it's better I don't have one."[†]

My Forbidden Past (1951), made on loan-out to RKO, is a steamy tale of adultery, notorious antecedents, a mysterious inheritance, and an impecunious, aristocratic family embroiled in soap opera goings-on beside the bayous of New Orleans. Robert Mitchum is a noble medical researcher jilted by Gardner; he soon reappears with a bride (Janis Carter). This enrages Gardner who sicks her ne'er-do-well cousin, Melvyn Douglas, on the flirtatious lady. During a tryst, Douglas accidentally causes Carter's death, but Mitchum is accused. Gardner confesses her part in the sordid episode, and the film ends with an exonerated Mitchum consoling Gardner, suggesting a

[*] Joe Hyams, *Look*, Nov. 27 and Dec. 11, 1956

[†] Rona Jaffe, *Good Housekeeping*, March 1961

MY FORBIDDEN PAST (1951). With Robert Mitchum

MY FORBIDDEN PAST (1951). With Melvyn Douglas

reconciliation in the future.

Director Robert Stevenson tries to impose some style on this melodramatic hodge-podge, but the most he can manage is to dwell briefly on Halloween revels and the Creole accents of some atmospheric "darkies." For the rest, his camera lingers admiringly on Gardner's face; framed in feathers and jewels, clad in her wasp-waisted period gowns, she has never been lovelier. There's not much she can do to lend credibility to this calculating minx, so she utters Barbara Beaurevel's impassioned speeches in an attractively breathy voice and looks suitably heartbroken when events take several turns for the worse. Mitchum, burly and self-sacrificing, meanders through the film scarcely bothering to act. The only one who attempts a performance is Douglas, who puts more effort into his role as the oily, feckless roué than it deserves.

Universal had filmed Edna Ferber's *Show Boat* twice before, in 1929 and 1936. MGM's version, made by the Arthur Freed unit, with a new screenplay by John Lee Mahin, changed certain essentials, keeping Magnolia and Ravenal younger when they reunite and making Julie the instrument of their meeting. Judy Garland was Freed's first choice for the role of Julie, the half-caste singer. Lena Horne, who is partly black, probably would have been perfect in the role, and when Gardner tested for Julie she mouthed her song to a record made by Horne.

"There wasn't much enthusiasm about Ava, even making the test," recalls director George Sidney. "The studio was dead against it. But I was determined. I *knew* she would be Julie." In fact, the test was very good and she was finally assigned to the film. Gardner was determined to use her own voice, which vocal coach Roger Edens found entirely lacking in the qualities Julie should have, deciding that it was thin, hesitant and weak. But Sidney took a chance. "I thought, 'Well, let's try it.' She half-sang, half-spoke the lines and it was deeply moving. The whole unit clapped as she finished and she started to cry. At the last moment the studio made us replace her singing voice with that of a professional singer, Annette Warren. And was she upset!" Gardner does sing on the cast album and her voice is, in reality, expressive and warm, albeit small, just the right vocal characteristics to accompany Gardner's performance, her first as an ill-fated half-caste.

The Sidney/Freed/Mahin *Show Boat* (1951) takes place in a land of happy darkies, cotton and Technicolored Mississippi River atmosphere overlaid with the elements of

SHOW BOAT (1951). As Julie

purest soap opera: the romance and marriage of Magnolia (Kathryn Grayson) and Gaylord Ravenal (Howard Keel) which can't survive financial hardship, and the parallel story of Julie LaVerne and Stephen Baker (Robert Sterling), kicked off the Cotton Blossom by the sheriff when their mixed marriage is discovered. Julie slides downhill rapidly, becoming a lush and a cabaret singer who, years later, runs into Ravenal on a river boat. By this time she is a tramp, still beautiful, but exhausted, heartbroken and bitter. And this is Gardner's finest scene. Demanding, "Give me a neat rye, just to get my courage up," she proceeds to tell Keel off for abandoning the pregnant Grayson. Haunted, sallow, aware of what she has become, Gardner pleads, "Don't ever tell her you saw me like this." Then, having effected the reunion, she smiles, watching the show boat slide down the river as William Warfield reprises "Old Man River."

In her earlier scenes, Gardner is cheerful and exultantly in love, exclaiming, "Can't Help Lovin' that Man" to Grayson; later, propping herself against a cafe piano, she sings "Bill," evocatively and tenderly, using this song to reveal her feelings for Sterling, who has left her by this time.

The 1936 James Whale version of *Show Boat*, which starred Irene Dunne, Allan Jones, Paul Robeson and Helen Morgan, is definitely superior to the Sidney opus, but interestingly, Morgan, although she does, of course, use her own singing voice, is in several ways not as satisfying a Julie as Gardner. Morgan is plump, almost dumpy, and Whale doesn't direct her to get the maximum emotional impact from either of her songs. "Can't Help Lovin' That Man" is taken at a more rapid pace, so that the yearning quality Gardner has, leaning against the rail of the Cotton Blossom, is missing, and the last chorus is shared with Hattie McDaniel, Robeson and Dunne, who camps it up, very charmingly and amusingly, with a shuffle. The shuffle is used, in modified style, by Gardner and Grayson, so it's more of a *pas de deux* between chums. After she's sung "Bill" at the Trocadero, Morgan simply disappears from the narrative; there's less of a tragic feeling about her because she isn't as visible as Gardner. Gardner's reappearance at the end reminds audiences that she's the victim of a cruel social injustice, and using her as the means of reuniting Keel and Grayson gives her a sort of vicarious triumph over the romantic unhappiness she and the other couple have been subjected to.

Gardner herself has the last, and best, word about her experience in

SHOW BOAT (1951). With Robert Sterling

the film: "I really tried in *Show Boat* but that was MGM crap. Typical of what they did to me there. I wanted to sing those songs —hell, I've still got a Southern accent—and I really thought Julie should sound a little like a Negro since she's supposed to have Negro blood. Christ, those songs like "Bill" shouldn't sound like an opera. I made a damn good track of the songs and they said, 'Ava, are you outta your head?' Then they got [Warren]. They substituted her voice for mine, and now in the movie my Southern twang stops talking and her soprano starts singing—hell, what a mess. They . . . ended up with crap. I still get royalties on the records I did."

As Columbia Pictures had made a celluloid queen out of a Greek goddess by casting Rita Hayworth as Terpsichore in *Down to Earth*, MGM next cast Gardner as the legendary Pandora, the woman Zeus sent as a curse to mortal man because Prometheus had stolen fire from heaven. Zeus gave her a box from which all human ills, except hope, escaped. In scenarist/producer/director Albert Lewin's view a modern Pandora's existence is a curse on that small segment of humanity which lives and plays near Tossa del Mar on the Spanish coast of the thirties.

The screenplay of *Pandora and the Flying Dutchman* (1951) sounds like the feverish dream of a romantic visionary. Lewin, like Joseph L. Mankiewicz, another of Gardner's directors, has encrusted his story with his predilections and obsessions: in this case, quotations from the Rubaíyát of Omar Khayyám and Matthew Arnold combined with some heavy symbolism surrounding the interwoven legends of Pandora and the same flying Dutchman who inspired Richard Wagner's opera.

Gardner, as Pandora Reynolds, is a willful, selfish nightclub singer engaged to Nigel Patrick, a racing car driver. He, in turn, is loved by Sheila Sim, the niece of Harold Warrender who broods and comments on the events like a Greek chorus. Small wonder, for he is, in fact, a classical scholar. *Pandora* is but one of many of Gardner's films partially spoiled by a narration that is either superfluous or pretentious, and the solemn premonitions Warrender utters are both. Gardner is intrigued by the arrival of a strange yacht in the harbor and swims out to greet the newcomer. She finds James Mason (as Hendrick van der Zee) painting her portrait as Pandora, box in hand. In the course of delving into the mysteries of the past, Warrender asks Mason to translate a manuscript in archaic Dutch which turns out to be Mason's own story, the chronicle of the seemingly unfaith-

SHOW BOAT (1951). With Howard Keel

PANDORA AND THE FLYING DUTCHMAN (1951).
With Marius Goring and Nigel Patrick

ful wife (also Gardner, which explains her face in the portrait) he killed, his blasphemous outrage at his trial, the death he escapes, and the curse which carries him around the world seeking salvation through the love of a woman who cares enough to die for him, and whose love will permit him to find the peace of death.

Gardner and Mason fall in love, but he rejects her, not wanting her to sacrifice her life for him. When he believes Mason is about to leave, Warrender gives the translation to Gardner, who rushes to Mason's yacht. Mason's yacht is becalmed and the lovers are united at last in death as a sudden squall capsizes the vessel.

The film's emphasis is on Gardner's casual destructiveness. She first spots the yacht just as Patrick, to satisfy her whim and secure her promise of marriage, pushes his beloved racing car over a cliff. Gardner is infuriated at finding her face and name in Mason's painting and smears over her image. A dilettante, a member of Gardner's entourage (Marius Goring), commits suicide because he cannot have her, and she indirectly causes the death of matador Mario Cabre. Cabre, in love with Gardner, stabs Mason in the belief that, with this obstacle removed, she will be his. Still alive, Mason appears the next day at the bullring where an astonished Cabre is fatally gored by the bull. But

PANDORA AND THE FLYING DUTCHMAN (1951).
As Pandora Reynolds

through her love for Mason, Gardner reforms and becomes the woman Mason has sought for over three hundred years. Spiritually purified, she is no longer an insatiable thrill-seeker, but a woman willing, not merely to sublimate herself for her lover's benefit, but to join him in suicide.

The narration Lewin wrote for Warrender is a kind of intoxicated gibberish, full of doom and foreboding. Unfortunately, this mood is carried over to Gardner's role, which should be that of a capricious, headstrong siren, not that of a woman given to reflection or doubts. Indeed, it is precisely during those moments when Gardner is required to act as though she's thinking that she is least effective. She's assured, calm and gracious with men she can charm, but sounds like a child interrupting the grown-ups when she's with her intellectual superiors. Gardner is required to play Pandora as a gorgeous somnambulist who has her animated moments—those in which she wrecks the lives of those around her—then lapses into a state of passive receptivity. She is most evocative singing (in her own voice) "How Am I to Know?" as an expression of Pandora's yearning for true love and the wisdom to recognize it.

Yet, Gardner is more than a frivolous and shallow woman.

When she gazes at Mason's painting, she tells him wistfully, "It's what I'd like to be. Why am I not like that?" She wants to be better than she is, but until she falls in love with Mason, Gardner has no incentive to change. Mason's quest provides Gardner with the moral resolve to give meaning to her life. Twenty-four years after the film was made Mason commented: "Only two features of this film now stand up these many years later: the superb cinematography of Jack Cardiff and the resulting embellishment of Ava Gardner's great natural beauty."

Mason plays van der Zee with a somber intensity and makes Lewin's speechifying both moving and significant—as though one were supposed to believe his fancifully augmented story. Even though his role is a forbiddingly gloomy one, he is surprisingly successful and his long speech about "seeking the woman faithful and fair" willing to die for him conveys the Dutchman's eternal anguish at being both cast out of mortal society and denied the luxury of death.

In *Lone Star* (1952) Clark Gable, playing a cattle breeder and free lance soldier-of-fortune, tries to enlist Sam Houston's support for the United States' annexation of Texas. Gable encounters Broderick Crawford who hopes for a treaty with Mexico which will enable

PANDORA AND THE FLYING DUTCHMAN (1951).
With James Mason

LONE STAR (1952). With Clark Gable

him to become President of the greatly expanded Republic of Texas. Gardner plays Crawford's lady friend, Martha Ronda, the editor of the *Austin Blade*, who falls for Gable.

Gable is his customary rakish, charming self, the kind of man who, when rebuked for admiring Gardner instead of sticking to his mission, replies, "I just believe in living a balanced life—a little of this, a little of that." Gardner is not especially convincing as an editor; she's better singing "Lovers Were Meant to Cry" to Gable on a picturesque patio.

The ads called it "The battle for Texas and the battle of the sexes!" but *Lone Star* is really a vapid drama of no special merit which director Vincent Sherman fills with racing horses, chases, duels, fist fights and street brawls to cover its essential artificiality.

Even though Cynthia isn't in the original story, Ernest Hemingway asked Darryl F. Zanuck, the head of Twentieth Century-Fox, to cast Gardner in the film version of *The Snows of Kilimanjaro* (1952) which Casey Robinson was adapting for the screen. Robinson recalls: "I had written the part of Cynthia, the lost twenties girl, for Ava. I'd known her when she was young, a barefoot girl out of the tobacco fields. All of the qualities I saw in her when she was young had developed in just the right way for Cynthia. A

LONE STAR (1952). With Clark Gable

THE SNOWS OF KILIMANJARO (1952). With Gregory Peck

kind of doomed character . . . . But one who had the capacity to stick out her chin and say 'Give it to me.' And to do it with a kind of pathetic laugh. It was the right role for her, and it launched her as a very great international star."

Gardner had always responded well to a strong director whom she felt she could trust. Given her own insecurities, her ego needed the reinforcement that a veteran could give her. Henry King was just such a veteran and he remembers her involvement with the role of Cynthia: "No one else could have given it the sensitivity, the bruised quality, that Ava imparted to it. . . . she worked with a kind of desperate involvement and intensity that amazed me."

Robinson's *Kilimanjaro* tries sporadically to be faithful to the spirit of Hemingway's short story, but for the most part it fails. Gardner's Cynthia Green is the light of writer Harry Street's life, his one great love. They're part of that "lost generation" which lives and loafs in post-World War I Paris and which provides Street (Gregory Peck) with the title of his first book. (King and Gardner would film all this again five years later as *The Sun Also Rises*, from another Hemingway story.)

The money from his opus takes Peck and Gardner, his pregnant and adoring wife, a girl who describes herself by saying, "I'm only trying to be happy," on safari to Africa, where she is terrified and sickened by the killing. Believing she's a drag on Peck's creative energies and not wanting to tie him down, Gardner throws herself downstairs and loses the child. "Now we can go to the bullfights," she says with bitter resignation, and so they're off to Spain where she finally leaves him.

After some years of squandering his talent, Peck finds her during the Spanish Civil War—he's fighting and she's an ambulance driver. But a bomb blast pins her under the vehicle and they're reconciled only briefly. Saying, "I could be dying and if you touched me, I'd turn giddy," she proceeds to expire.

Peck then turns to a life of ease which finds him laid up, awaiting help for a leg wound, on safari once more, with his second wife, Susan Hayward. In Hemingway's story, it's implied that he dies, but here he is rescued in time for medical help to save him.

Gardner tries hard to be a "lost" good-time girl, seeking security and a home, and she is effective in her death scene, but for the most part her role is meaningless, serving only to pad out what was a *short* story and underscore the purposelessness of the life Peck comes to lead by representing the "normal" values he rejects. In spite of this, Gardner said she was happy playing Cynthia: "I really felt comfortable in that part. I could understand the girl I played so well. It wasn't like

THE SNOWS OF KILIMANJARO (1952). With Gregory Peck

RIDE, VAQUERO! (1953). With Robert Taylor

some of the other parts I've had. This girl wasn't a tramp or a bitch or a real smart cooky. She was a good average girl with normal impulses. I didn't have to pretend." Peck is appropriately self-pitying, but no more a Hemingway hero than was Tyrone Power in *The Sun Also Rises*. (Peck did better by Hemingway in the 1947 *Macomber Affair*.)

Bernard Herrmann created a musical score richer and more evocative than the drama which it highlighted, in particular some sensuous jazz for the party scene in which Gardner and Peck meet. Director King wisely focused his camera on the striking African scenery and the picturesque back streets of Paris, so that the muddled and unhappy characters in the foreground at least had attractive locales in which to suffer.

Ride, Vaquero! (1953) is set in post-Civil War Texas, where Howard Keel brings his bride (Gardner as Cordelia Cameron) to the homestead he's built. A bandit chief (Anthony Quinn) destroys the ranch as a warning to Keel and other settlers, whereupon Keel determines to stick it out and strike back. MGM, noted more for casting to type than against it, took the unusual step of assigning Robert Taylor to the role of Quinn's foster brother and henchman, who symbolically trades his black hat for a white one when he falls for Gardner. Quinn wounds an unarmed Keel, but is prevented from dispatching him altogether by Taylor, at which point Taylor and Quinn shoot each other in their tracks, dropping to the floor simultaneously.

John Farrow's direction is erratic, alternating slam-bang assaults on ranchers and townsfolk with static confrontations between the principals. Frank Fenton's script provides a meaty role only for Quinn who plays Jose Esqueda as a jovial cutthroat who gargles with wine and takes sadistic pleasure in making life intolerable for everyone. Certainly, no purpose is served by having Taylor, once Gardner is in his arms, smack her for trying to kiss him, because his code of ethics (the code of a vaquero, or cowboy) is offended. Gardner has a large share in the activities, but there is little to be gained from watching her, or anyone else perform, or indeed, from watching *Ride, Vaquero!*

For Gardner, the most memorable aspect of making the film was its miserable location in hot, airless Kanab, Utah where she and all concerned were stifled by the area's red dust. But better things were coming, by coincidence relating to *Red Dust*, not that of Kanab, but of the 1932 film which had starred Clark Gable, Jean Harlow and

Mary Astor. John Lee Mahin rewrote his own screenplay, which he'd adapted from Wilson Collison's play, updating the original to the fifties and changing the locale from an Indo-Chinese rubber plantation to an African safari. He also altered the frank sexual chemistry which had existed between Harlow and Gable to a relationship still lusty, but more acceptable to a Hollywood dominated by the production code.

The Harlow of *Red Dust* and the Gardner of *Mogambo* (1953) are more than just stranded sisters under the skin—they're blood relations. Their parts are as closely related as Gable's Dennis Carson is to his Vic Marswell, with the exception that Harlow is explicitly more of a tramp. When Gardner has to explain how she became an international playgirl, the companion of maharajahs, she tells how she lost her husband in the war and just went to pieces, showing, as she wryly puts it, "great strength of character." Their dialogue is the same without being identical and Gardner is more inclined to observe the amenities; instead of having Gable stare down at Harlow's nude body in a rain barrel, he is forced to keep his distance when he spies Gardner using his shower. On all counts, though, Gardner is as slangy, as hip-wiggling and as hip as Harlow was.

Her Eloise "Honey Bear" Kelly is also a good guy, the sort of girl the screen Gable was always on the lookout for—and the sort of part Gardner played best. She's a dame who says, "Look buster, don't get overstimulated with me," yet prances around the animal compound in her high heels and leaves her bra where Gable can stare quizzically at it. "Honey Bear" knows what she's up to and plays her cards straight. The appearance of Grace Kelly, as anthropologist Donald Sinden's wife, puts a crimp in her plans, but she respects Gable's obvious attraction to Kelly and keeps her distance, letting the relationship—not the "affair" of the 1932 film, but rather a series of scenic walks through the African bush which inevitably leads to a clinch—develop as it will. The dénouement is the same, as Kelly pumps a bullet into Gable when she thinks he's been toying with her, while Gardner comes up with a fast excuse for Sinden to get Kelly off the hook and put the blame on Gable. Gardner is about to shove off, once and for all, when Gable calls her back; she jumps overboard and wades happily ashore, having tamed her white hunter at last.

Twice Gable tells Gardner, "You're all right," and the frank admiration he was so expert at projecting finds in Gardner a target worth aiming at. The Astor role has

MOGAMBO (1953).
As Eloise (Honey Bear) Kelly

MOGAMBO (1953). With Clark Gable

MOGAMBO (1953). With Clark Gable

been changed, however, so that Kelly has to play the wife as a twittering simp, cooing over the adorable animals and acting like an all-purpose curse on the expedition. This makes Gable's affection for her hard to comprehend, especially with the relaxed and available Gardner only one tent away.

Eloise "Honey Bear" Kelly ranks with Maria Vargas, Victoria Jones and Moira Davidson, of *The Barefoot Contessa, Bhowani Junction* and *On the Beach*, respectively, as one of Gardner's few worthwhile parts, and Gardner is fully up to playing her. Director John Ford wisely keeps her in the foreground where she can distract attention from Kelly and Sinden, who, by

contrast and by any standards, are as boring a pair as any safari ever harbored. Chewing gum or standing in her negligee against a lighted doorway, Gardner is enough to start any African tom-tom thumping loudly, much less Gable's virile heart. Gardner is also ingenuous and sweet, two qualities not often found in her emotional makeup on screen. "Hey, a kangaroo," she exclaims cheerily as a hippopotamus flounders in the river, then makes light of her own ignorance, observing, "Everything but a zipper," when Sinden explains the difference between the two species.

Like the role she played in *The Hucksters* against a younger, but no more vigorous, Gable, Gardner

KNIGHTS OF THE ROUND TABLE (1953). With Mel Ferrer

is a good-time girl, a perfect partner for the kind of man who likes to love 'em and leave 'em; but here she proves to be something more important—the kind of woman the man doesn't want to leave.

Many directors tried to capitalize, as Lewin and Mankiewicz did, on Gardner's womanliness, on the sensuality that was as natural to her as breathing. Interestingly, the only director who succeeded completely, John Ford, was the one who almost ignored this aspect of her persona in favor of her largely untapped gift for comedy. Not that Ford disregards her feline femininity; he underplays it so that Gardner's sexuality is part of her personality, not the primary reason for

her existence. And this is what makes Honey Bear such a memorable character; she has more than one or two dimensions: she's a woman with a past, but not a femme fatale, she's very much *of* the present, and she's artless without being naive.

Gardner's sister, Inez Grimes, declared that "It's the only picture in which I ever liked Ava. I knew when I saw it that the director had let her improvise some of the dialogue. Some of the expressions I had often heard her use in family conversation."

But this cooperative air which allowed Gardner to do her best work was not arrived at easily. Usually autocratic and taciturn, Ford treated

KNIGHTS OF THE ROUND TABLE (1953). With Robert Taylor

Gardner as he did all but the inner circle of his co-workers and friends—like a paid pariah. But one day Ford called her aside and complimented her, and Gardner speaks warmly of him: "From that moment on, he was wonderful, directing me, talking to me, making me understand. I guess that's how he works. He has to be top man—and he should be. He just wanted to make sure I knew it."

Nominated for an Academy Award for *Mogambo*, Gardner was reportedly relieved when she lost to Audrey Hepburn in *Roman Holiday*. After all, winning a Oscar implies a serious approach to one's *métier*, an attitude the public Gardner was loathe to admit the private Gardner possessed, no matter how much she complained about the roles MGM assigned her.

Gardner's reward for the excellent work she'd done in *Mogambo* was to be sent to England by MGM for *Knights of the Round Table* (1953), the studio's first Cinema-Scope production. The reward was more like a punishment, for in seeking to capitalize on the success of co-star Robert Taylor's and director Richard Thorpe's collaboration on the 1952 *Ivanhoe*, the studio gave less care and attention to the vehicle in which they worked, thinking perhaps that the novelty of the Band-Aid-shaped screen could overcome what script and production lacked. *Round Table* tips its helmet in the direction of Malory's "Le Morte D'Arthur," drawing on the legend of Excalibur, the enmity of Morgan Le Fay and Modred for Arthur, and the wise old magician, Merlin, pottering around uttering sage but obscure advice.

Gardner plays Guinevere, rescued by Lancelot (Taylor) from some wayward knights en route to her marriage to Arthur (Mel Ferrer) at Camelot. Lancelot is made Queen's Companion, a bodyguard of somewhat elevated status, a circumstance Modred (Stanley Baker) and Morgan (Anne Crawford) believe they can use against Arthur and to their advantage, perhaps dividing the knights of the round table. Eventually, the deadly pair succeed, accusing Guinevere and Lancelot of treason against the throne. This version cleans the narrative up somewhat; the couple are guilty of no more than some straying glances and a single kiss, so goodhearted Arthur simply banishes Lancelot from the kingdom and Guinevere to a convent, then settles down to a series of civil wars which destroy the round table and eventually kill him. Lancelot returns to England in time for Arthur's dying benediction and, after dispatching Modred to an early grave, brings a message of forgiveness to Guinevere.

Where the Taylor/Thorpe *Ivan-*

THE BAREFOOT CONTESSA (1954). As Maria Vargas

THE BAREFOOT CONTESSA (1954). With Edmond O'Brien

hoe had been a genuinely exciting conflict between the hero and De-Bois Guilbert, with Guilbert played by George Sanders as a flawed but complex and comprehensible individual ruled by an uncontrollable passion, the Lancelot/Arthur conflict with Modred looks like a squabble among three boys in a sandbox. Ferrer, who does the best with the material at hand, nevertheless affects a "heavy, heavy hangs the head that wears the crown" attitude, which, along with the general turgidity of the action and pace, is unfortunate. Gardner stands around as though posing for a tapestry, looking agitated or amused as befits the occasion; her part is written for a cardboard queen, and, when compared with other versions of the legend, for example the role Alan Jay Lerner later provided for Vanessa Redgrave in the film of *Camelot*, Gardner would have been justified in suing for robbery.

That year Gardner had an unbilled walk-on as herself in *The Band Wagon*. She arrives at Grand Central Station on the same train as Fred Astaire and is greeted by the press. She poses cheerily for photographers and chats with Astaire. The real Gardner, in the same situation, would doubtless have sworn lustily and kicked the gentlemen in the slats.

When writer/director Joseph L. Mankiewicz decided to indulge himself by making *The Barefoot Contessa* (1954), he had an enviable string of Hollywood successes behind him, including *All About Eve*, for which he'd won the writing and directing Academy Awards, *Five Fingers* and *Julius Caesar*. He was in a unique position to do exactly as he pleased, and he did. Everyone wanted to play the Rita Hayworth-like Maria Vargas, but Mankiewicz held out for Gardner, who experienced MGM's usual resistance at being allowed to do a project *she* was interested in. "I just had to play it," she told the director. "Hell, Joe, I'm not an actress, but I think I understand this girl. She's a lot like me."

Gardner's salary had gone up steadily over the years, not to the astronomical figures some actresses achieved, but to respectable sums; likewise the fees Metro got for her loan-out services. Mankiewicz told her that MGM's terms for her were $200,000 plus ten percent of the gross after the first million. Bogart got $100,000 and Gardner a mere $60,000, at which she commented icily, "That's Metro. They'll louse you every time." She was doubly anxious to get away from Hollywood—to Italy, where *Contessa* was filmed—because her marriage to Sinatra was disintegrating. He had won his Oscar for *From Here to Eternity* and was back on top again, and apparently didn't need her loyalty and

THE BAREFOOT CONTESSA (1954). With Humphrey Bogart

Gardner in the mid-fifties

support any more.

Contessa's story concerns a Spanish nightclub dancer made into a movie star by Warren Stevens, playing a millionaire resembling Gardner's old friend, Howard Hughes, and by Humphrey Bogart as a philosophical writer/director obviously modeled on Mankiewicz himself, and as Bogart put it, ". . . after most of my friends who are ex-drunks." Marius Goring was a lecherous playboy modeled on Porfirio Rubirosa and Edmond O'Brien's role as a sweaty, double-talking press agent was said to be founded on Johnny Meyer, an associate of Hughes.

Maria's story is told in flashbacks from the focal point of her funeral by Bogart, O'Brien and Rossano Brazzi as the Count she marries after many affairs with men she euphemizes as her "cousins." The funeral is dominated by a statue of Gardner as the Contessa Torlato-Favrini, barefoot and very much resembling her earlier incarnation as Venus. The multiple flashbacks take the spectator from Madrid to Hollywood to Italy and detail each event in Gardner's meteoric rise to stardom, including the rehabilitation of her mentor and friend, Bogart, and ending with her marriage to Brazzi, who reveals himself, on their wedding night, to be impotent, the result of a war wound. Gardner immediately takes up with a hot-eyed chauffeur and prepares to present the Count with an heir to the moribund family name. Bogart, who has characterized Brazzi as a neurotic, bitter man finishing life on his own terms, tells Gardner her bridegroom won't be happy at the news. But Gardner, whom Bogart calls a "Spanish Cinderella," cursed with an inability to face the truth about herself or about life, denies this. Bogart's opinion is vindicated when, shortly thereafter, Brazzi kills Gardner and her lover.

The Barefoot Contessa is a potpourri into which Mankiewicz funneled everything he ever wanted to say about Hollywood, and the international cafe society which is its European equivalent. In its way the film was as personal and close to him as *Citizen Kane* was to his older brother, Herman Mankiewicz, and Orson Welles, or *Grand Illusion* was to Jean Renoir. There are endless soliloquies by every member of the cast, brilliant flashes of insight and equally sharp, sardonic dialogue. But it's uneven; for each bright segment, there's a correspondingly dull portion to be endured, and one or two impossible performances. Brazzi is pretentious and self-conscious; doom is written in every furrow of his brow. Goring has been directed to play the millionaire as an egotistical fancy-man. On the other hand, Bo-

gart is the best spokesman Mankiewicz could have picked for his point of view—ironic, sincere and loyal. O'Brien deservedly won an Academy Award for his role as Oscar Muldoon, Stevens' sycophantic aide.

Gardner, whose early life might well have served as a model for the role she plays, gives a performance like the film's reviews—mixed. She begins the film with traces of a Spanish accent; soon she's dropped it altogether, occasionally snarling a remark in idiomatic Spanish, which she handles very well. She is enormously impressive in a scene without dialogue, narrated by O'Brien, in which she testifies at her father's trial for the murder of her mother. Simply, with dignity and great fervor, she details the reasons for her mother's death. Gardner is most believable as a physical presence, the woman who embodies the qualities O'Brien describes: "Whatever it is, you name it. Whether you're born with it or catch it from a public drinking cup, Maria had it." Superbly photographed by Jack Cardiff (also the cinematographer of *Pandora and the Flying Dutchman*), she is indeed, as the film's ads claimed, "The world's most magnificent animal!"

One scene serves to emphasize the carnal quality Gardner emanates. She dances barefoot, in an apache outfit—tight sweater and cheap satin skirt—at a gypsy camp, to Mario Nascimbene's haunting, deeply sensuous "Theme from *The Barefoot Contessa*." As she weaves around her partner, eluding his grasp, giving her utmost concentration to the steps, Gardner's dance sums up her role: the woman who can't be possessed except on her own terms and whose mere presence is almost unbearably intoxicating. It echoes her first "appearance" in the film, her dance in a Madrid nightclub where her performance is reflected entirely in the expressions of lust, admiration, etc. that cross the faces of the spectators. Gardner's presence is suggested only by a moving spotlight, the sound of castinets and a swaying beaded curtain, but these and the reactions of the patrons are enough to suggest that something remarkable and profoundly affecting has occurred.

It's significant that when she makes up her mind to go to Hollywood, Gardner asks Bogart if he can teach her to act, indicating that she won't be content to be simply a "star." Gardner, who has always derided her talent, has given many expert performances which reveal her as more than a star—an actress of ability and persuasive gifts. It seems certain that if she had been less insecure and taken her ability more seriously, she would have had a more interesting and rewarding career, one of which she could have been proud. In *Contessa*, however, she is saddled with too much cumbersome and awkwardly phrased dialogue. She seems to be having difficulty in reaching the essence of Maria and extracting from herself some emotional quality or personal experience she can relate to the part.

Bogart didn't like Gardner and didn't try to hide it—off screen. He purposely blew his lines when he thought their scenes together weren't going well, so that Mankiewicz would have to shoot a retake. His judgment may have been correct and to Bogart may belong some of the credit Gardner got for her portrayal. But he stepped aside when it came to the press, telling the picture's publicist, David Hanna, "Let's face it, all the interest is going to be in Ava Gardner. She's the news, not me."

In April of 1954, when filming was completed, Gardner suffered an acute attack of gallstones and spent over a month in a Madrid hospital recuperating. Her constant companion was Luis Miguel Dominguin, at the time Spain's greatest matador, himself recovering from a severe goring in the ring. He brought Ernest Hemingway, who was staying at the Palace Hotel, with his wife Mary and friend A.E. Hotchner, to see Gardner in the hospital. Hemingway had admired *The Killers*, despite its departure from the original, as the best film version of his work, and had ridiculed Gardner's 1952 film as *The Snows of Zanuck*.

Hemingway found Gardner, attended by nuns, screaming into the phone, refusing via long distance to play Ruth Etting in *Love Me or Leave Me*: "Great part? I stand there mouthing words like a goddam goldfish while you're piping in some goddam dubbed voice! I said a *dramatic* part, and you send me Ruth Etting! It's no wonder I've got this attack. I ought to send you the bill!"

Gardner hung up, and in an abrupt about-face, greeted Hemingway graciously, "Sit here on the bed, Papa, and talk to me. I'm absolutely floored you could come." When Hemingway asked if she was going to settle in Spain, Gardner replied, "Yes, I sure am. I'm just a country girl at heart. I don't like New York or Paris. I'd love to live here permanently. What have I got to go back to? I have no car, no house, nothing. Sinatra's got nothing either. All I got out of any of my marriages was the two years Artie Shaw financed on an analyst's couch."

Her relationship with Dominguin convinced Gardner that she should terminate her marriage to Sinatra, and fully recuperated, she

BHOWANI JUNCTION (1956). As Victoria Jones

departed for Lake Tahoe in order to qualify for a Nevada divorce. She was also a temporarily free agent; Metro had suspended her for refusing *Love Me or Leave Me*. Although Gardner stated that "Sinatra and I aren't going to be together again—ever," she left the state without picking up her decree because financial arrangements between them had not been completed. Gardner wanted Sinatra to return some money she had lent him when he was in a bad financial position. Otherwise, as she put it, "He'll take what he has and I'll take what I have." The divorce became official in 1957. As late as December of 1954 Gardner wanted to make *St. Louis Woman*, from the 1946 Johnny Mercer-Harold Arlen Broadway musical, with Sinatra. She even signed a contract with MGM for an additional year in order to do the film, but the plans eventually came to nothing. Earlier, in 1953, Metro had purchased the William I. Wellman novel, "The Female," about a beautiful girl's struggle to rise from her lowly station in sixth century Constantinople, as a vehicle for Gardner. The film was never made.

She embarked upon a promotional tour for *The Barefoot Contessa* with David Hanna, who later became her manager and wrote a book about the middle part of her career called "Ava, a Portrait of a Star." The unruly mob that greeted her in Rio de Janeiro made international headlines and it also made Gardner black and blue, mauling and pinching her until she was reduced to hysterics.

Once the lengthy tour was over, Gardner settled down in a modest house in Palm Springs where Hanna, visiting to discuss *Contessa*, noticed a young man who was always hanging around. The man was named Bill and he was a professional "spy," assigned by Howard Hughes to report on Gardner's every activity and conversation. Gardner told Hanna that Hughes' attentions, as welcome as they may have been at the time, were probably the one factor which had taken Dominguin, who had visited her in Nevada, away from her for good.

Gardner's difficulties with the press weren't over with the end of her marriage to Frank Sinatra. In 1955, she posed with Sammy Davis, Jr. for a cover of the magazine, *Our World*. Some of the pictures, including one of her holding Davis's hand, later appeared in the scandal journal *Confidential* and shocked many residents of her North Carolina home town. As a friend of Gardner's, Bernadette Hoyle, told Joe Hyams of *Look* magazine, "The thing no one in Smithfield could understand was how Ava could pose with Davis for a picture." As a local store owner put it:

BHOWANI JUNCTION (1956). With Bill Travers

BHOWANI JUNCTION (1956). With Stewart Granger

"Ava's a Southerner. How'n hell could she sit holding hands with a nigger?" An MGM representative said of the mail she received because of the incident: "The things they called her were disgraceful."

Garder refused to sue *Confidential* because the suit would cause even more publicity, and defended her behavior by stating: "I'm not ashamed of my friendship with Sammy. I think he's a great artist and I feel there's no color line when it comes to talent or friends."

Gardner had settled her differences with Metro and signed a new contract, one which not only called for substantially more money than ever, but which gave her some measure of control over her films and the right to make them in Europe so she could reap some financial advantages from not paying taxes in the United States. The first movie under the new terms was *Bhowani Junction* (1956), and when she visited the studio with Hanna before leaving, she took a good look at the factory Louis B. Mayer had ruled so ruthlessly for so long, and where she had spent so many hours, both profitable and unrewarding. "It's no great shakes now," she asserted, "but it was a damned sight better when the old man was around. I never liked him very much but at least you knew where you stood. This joint's come down a lot in the world."

The location scenes for *Bhowani*

Junction were shot in Lahore, Pakistan because India's tax collectors wanted too large a portion of the film's profits, and because the Indian government was leery of its twin subjects—India's recent upheaval and the Anglo-Indian leading character. Pakistan waived nearly all taxes and provided the all-important cooperation and participation of the 13th Battalion Frontier Force and the Northwestern Railway.

The political background of the film is the India of 1947 when the British were preparing to withdraw and the country was in turmoil. This unrest was fostered by the non-violent Congress Party, and the Indians were incited to riot by a

rabid Communist faction. Under the command of a British Army Colonel (Stewart Granger) who leads the troops at Bhowani Junction is WAC I Subaltern Victoria Jones (Gardner), an Anglo-Indian half-caste, or "chee-chee" in vulgar slang. Victoria is a tormented woman, unsure of her identity, and incapable of making up her mind as to which world she prefers. She is first involved with a fellow half-blood, played by Bill Travers, but breaks with him because of his emotional pro-white bias and inability to look beyond the present. She next becomes engaged to an Indian (Francis Matthews), but is unable to wholeheartedly embrace his life style. Lastly, Victoria loves and

THE LITTLE HUT (1957). With David Niven and Stewart Granger

THE LITTLE HUT (1957). With Walter Chiari

agrees to marry the Colonel, but only if they remain in India. She feels that she must stay because of her failure to become either fully British or Indian. As she tells the Colonel, "I belong here, not as a phony Indian, not as a phony white, but as myself."

Director George Cukor's camera strays from Victoria/Gardner only to record the turbulent events which surround her and into which, despite her lack of strong political convictions, she is inextricably drawn, both professionally and personally. The political circumstances serve more as colorful panorama against which to pose Victoria's various moral crises, rather than having any intrinsic merit of their own.

Gardner has several scenes of extraordinary intensity and power in which her mature gifts as an actress are given greater scope than usual. With an intelligent script (by Sonya Levien and Ivan Moffat, from John Masters' novel) and meaningful dialogue, she rises to the challenge of doing justice to this complex and divided human being. In one sequence she argues vehemently with Travers over his blind worship of all things British. A whole range of expressions—rage, frustration, compassion—crosses her face in rapid succcssion, rather than the more customary frozen beauty she had been required to exhibit in the past. With her hair loose and flying, her body bending free of the erect posture which had imprisoned her in earlier performances, Gardner is a figure of humane convictions and great emotional force.

Cukor focuses on the sensual aspect of Gardner, and men's reactions to her, responding to her face and figure as Mankiewicz and Lewin had before him. Kneeling in a Sikh temple, her body swathed in a sari, she shows, in Cukor's extreme close-up, both her beauty and her doubts as she reels, then bolts, under the enormous pressure of her ambivalence.

Unfortunately, MGM divested *Bhowani Junction* of some of its erotic power by eliminating at least two sequences and adding a narration, spoken by Granger, annoy-ingly emphasizing and reiterating Gardner's split consciousness. This was not the first Gardner film to be spoiled, at least partially, by this superfluous and redundant narrative technique. *The Killers* and *The Barefoot Contessa* were her only pictures which used this device successfully.

One of the excised sequences was a love scene between Travers and Gardner. The second Cukor remembers as follows: "The scene on the train with the British colonel—she realizes she's attracted to him and her behavior becomes rather loose and sluttish. She takes his toothbrush [dipping it in scotch first] and cleans her teeth in front of him ... The picture was seri-

THE SUN ALSO RISES (1957). With Tyrone Power

ously oversimplified and made to look sentimental at moments—which it never originally was."

Cukor went further in his comments: "Stewart Granger was wrong as the colonel. I wanted Trevor Howard. Stewart Granger was just a movie star and he brought out the movie queen in Ava Gardner. She was good, but she and everything else would have been better with Trevor Howard." In another context, Cukor spoke admiringly of Gardner's work in the film: "She did everything herself, no matter how dangerous or strenuous—the kidnapping, the riots. She was black and blue most of the time, and Ava loathes physical violence. She was marvelously punctual and never complained even when it was clear the poor darling was *exhausted*. She was wonderful in the part."

Filming completed, Gardner did the thing she'd spoken of often and determinedly—she settled in Spain. She bought a house in La Moraleja, a suburb of Madrid, and moved in in December of 1955. Early in 1956 she flew to Palma, Majorca, where she met the celebrated English poet and author, Robert Graves. They became great friends, and he marked a passage, which seems remarkably biographical, in a book of his poetry for her:

"She speaks always in her
own voice

Even to strangers . . .
She is wild and innocent,
pledged to love
Through all disaster. . . ''

Gardner was still under contract to Metro, and since she'd rejected both *Love Me or Leave Me*, a decision she regretted because it had rejuvenated the slightly sagging career of Doris Day, and still another film, she consented to make *The Little Hut* (1957) with Stewart Granger (again) and an old friend from Hollywood, David Niven.

The film was made on sets which leave no doubt that the cast never left the studio, and Mark Robson, whose limited talents were better suited to strong dramatic fare, directed lethargically. The play by Andre Roussin was nothing special to begin with, but the premise—that the woman played by Gardner would inevitably have to be shared by the three robust males with whom she's stranded on a desert island—at least made sense. MGM bowdlerized the plot so that she successfully eludes everyone's grasp, including her husband's. Niven and Granger cavort around the island like two aging children, hoisting the British flag, dressing for dinner even though they're eating off leaves, and sharing Granger's shoes in the same querulous spirit Niven wants to share Granger's wife. Niven's plans are foiled

THE SUN ALSO RISES (1957). As Lady Brett Ashley

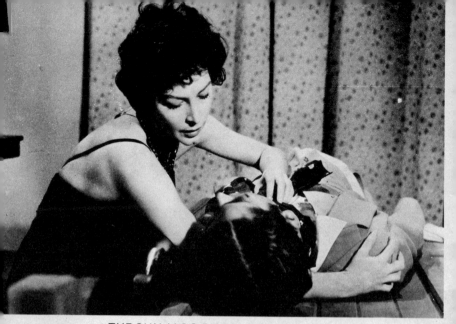

THE SUN ALSO RISES (1957). With Robert Evans

first by Granger's dog, then by the arrival of Walter Chiari, dressed in a fake "native" outfit and yelling "Boola, boola!" like an hysterical son of old Yale. Chiari turns out to be the chef, another survivor of the yachting accident that brought them to the island, and soon all four are rescued. Granger, who has neglected Gardner up until then, is so attentive that she becomes pregnant, thus thwarting forever Niven's plans for a permanent takeover.

The film is smarmy and tasteless; the general tone is one of pandering to an audience's most prurient expectations, then thwarting them with a nasty smile and a bamboo blind, sniggeringly lowered behind an amorously inclined Gardner. Granger patronizes Gardner by telling Niven, "She's extremely childlike and she's quite incapable of having a lover," then agrees to a divorce so Niven can "have" Gardner, while a record player she's managed to drag along plays "Everything I Have is Yours." Granger is smug, Niven looks simultaneously lovesick and uncomfortable, and Gardner is almost idiotically cheerful throughout.

Gardner, as usual, was mercilessly accurate in summing up what was wrong with her films, saying of *The Little Hut* that she "hated every minute of it. It was a lousy story. The director was awful. But

THE NAKED MAJA (1959). With Massimo Serato

what could I do? If I took another suspension they would keep me at Metro the rest of my life." In 1953, she had been similarly perspicacious in stating, of Hemingway's *The Sun Also Rises*, "Oh, I hope they don't try to make a movie out of that, because they couldn't, not without spoiling it." But, once more loaned to Fox for a Hemingway film with director Henry King, she played Lady Brett Ashley. She hadn't changed her mind when shooting was completed, asserting: "I don't think Hemingway is going to like what they did to his book. I think it got loused up somewhere along the line." And she was right.

Peter Viertel's adaptation, while including much of the scenic beauty of Paris and Pamplona (actually filmed in Morelia, Mexico when a miserable Spanish winter forced the company to change hemispheres) during the *feria*, omits much of Hemingway's "lost generation" feeling about going to hell in a taxi, about too much booze and not knowing how to live or what to live for. Errol Flynn, as Gardner's sodden and impecunious fiancé, comes closest to capturing this illusive spirit of prodigal, unhappy dissipation. With his puffy face, his ironic and argumentative manner, Flynn is perfect as the man Gardner leaves, first for a bullfighter (played with callow charm by Robert Evans, now better known as a Para-

mount Pictures chieftain), then to return to her first love, Tyrone Power.

A flashback early in the film depicts Gardner, a Red Cross nurse, tending Power in a hospital just as he discovers his World War I wound has left him impotent. The rest of the film chronicles the frustrated romance of the not-quite lovers, as well as Gardner's joyless partying and casual nymphomania, which always ends with Power comforting her in a taxi as they take up their unsatisfactory relationship once more.

Power plays Jake Barnes (as he had the hero of *The Razor's Edge*), as a philosophical onlooker, a receptacle for virtually any experience, and a part of any alliance people care to have with him. As a Hemingway hero, he's too stoical and doesn't convey the doomed aura the author's heroes ordinarily imparted, but Gardner does well as the predatory Lady Brett, accurately mirroring her dissatisfied promiscuity, and her selfish but ultimately anguished discontent. It's a role that presages the similarly unhappy Moira Davidson, who also can't have the man she loves, of *On the Beach* (1959). King's direction is commonplace, failing to capture both the genuine spirit of revelry and the pointless hedonism which characterized the real "lost generation" that whooped it up in the

THE NAKED MAJA (1959). As the Duchess of Alba

Paris of 1922.

Watching Gardner struggle through these unsatisfactory adaptations of Hemingway works prompts thoughts about a somewhat younger Gardner playing other "lost generation" heroines: Nicole in F. Scott Fitzgerald's *Tender is the Night* or Gloria in *The Beautiful and the Damned*. But by 1957 she was thirty-five and beginning to look her age. Gardner was always an exceptionally healthy and vibrant woman, but too many late hours and too much alcohol were starting to show in her face.

In October, 1957 Gardner and Walter Chiari, who had become a close friend, visited the Spanish ranch of Angelo Peralta, the famous breeder of bulls, whom Hemingway had introduced her to. She was teased into riding a horse—for the first time—and attempting *toreo a caballo*, bullfighting on horseback. Gardner fell from her horse, and her right cheek began to swell. Her injury was not taken seriously at first, but when it was, she was flown immediately to see Sir Archibald McIndoe, a renowned London plastic surgeon. She had suffered a hematoma, a blood clot which had formed inside her right cheek. McIndoe warned her not to have it operated on, saying that it would disappear of its own accord. And slowly the hematoma did vanish, but not before Gardner had been terrified of losing her looks, that photographable face which made her such a valuable commodity. She became extremely sensitive about the tiny lump, but it is virtually invisible in her subsequent films, and gradually she lost her irrational fear of any sort of accident.

The Naked Maja (1959) released by United Artists but cofinanced by Metro, which paid Gardner only $90,000 for starring in the film, was her last picture under her MGM contract. She told her biographer, David Hanna, "I wouldn't admit this to anyone else, but I'm afraid. I never worked for any other company. I never had another job. I hate their guts but for seventeen years they've been there and I just did what they told me to, going from one lousy picture to the other," a statement which reflects the ambivalance with which she colored all remarks connected with her career. In fact, not every picture she made for Metro had been "lousy," but, indeed, they had not been particularly zealous in taking care of their star, or making sure that her vehicles did her justice, or even helping her to find new challenges to her abilities. As a freelance she would make a few interesting films: *On the Beach, Seven Days in May* and *Night of the Iguana*, and thereafter make progressively fewer

THE NAKED MAJA (1959). With Anthony Franciosa

films, or appear in less prestigious projects.

The Naked Maja purports to chronicle the tumultuous historical era and flaming passions of the affair between Francisco Goya (Anthony Franciosa) and the Duchess of Alba (Gardner). The film is factually inaccurate, mixes its chronology, and compresses history to suit the exigencies of the filmmakers. At the time of the Spanish Inquisition, which figures prominently in the narrative, Goya had not yet painted Alba, but her portraits and the Church's infamies are blended in a melodramatic hodge-podge involving his supposed blasphemy. The real Goya was forty-nine when he painted Alba, hardly the hand-

some youth Franciosa depicts, and the actual Spanish court only rumored that Goya and Alba were lovers. In fact, Alba, her husband (she's a widow in the film) and Goya were close friends.

The film only suggests the ferocious idealism which guided Goya in his savage artistic attacks on the hypocrisy of the Church, the corruption of the court, and the misery of the Spanish people. The film is dominated by Gardner and Franciosa's mooningly banal romantic duologues or their misery when wrested from each other's arms by affairs of state, intrigues and death. Gardner's Alba dies of slow poison, and as Franciosa enters her chamber, sculptures of lovingly en-

ON THE BEACH (1959). As Moira Davidson

ON THE BEACH (1959). With Fred Astaire

twined cherubs frame the doorway, mirroring the postures Gardner and Franciosa are forever falling into. Her death scene carries strong echoes of Garbo's in *Camille* and Merle Oberon's Cathy in *Wuthering Heights*, with Franciosa supporting her as she tries to rise. "Look for me in every Spanish face," Gardner whispers, inspiring her lover even as she expires, collapsed on a divan.

Gardner almost doesn't have to act, since the moronic dialogue, by Norman Corwin and Giorgio Prosperi, gives her nothing worthwhile to say, although she tries very hard with the few lines that aren't laughable. Franciosa expends even more effort, playing Goya as a kind of

"Method" painter, but manages to give even less of a performance, and looks simply vigorous or haggard as necessary. The one scene that implies the erotic passion these fictional characters might have been capable of takes place in a café. As the sensuous music swells, their bodies curl around each other in a quasi-flamenco, ending as their faces, nearly touching, impart a heady amorous fervor to their *pas de deux*.

Cinematographer Giuseppe Rotunno fills the canvas of the screen to overflowing like a Goya painting and director Henry Koster tries to keep the action moving swiftly enough so the senselessness of the plot isn't too conspicuous. *Maja*

101

should have been filmed in Spain, but the influential descendants of the house of Alba prevented this, and only a few paintings and exteriors were actually shot there, the rest of the movie being made in Italy. The film's failure as drama is unfortunate, for Gardner is a natural—and perfect—odalisque, a female whose face and figure, like Helen of Troy's, could launch a thousand ships. By simply superimposing her face on a copy of the Goya original, the producers slighted both women. Gardner is more statuesque than Alba, but the real Alba was, after all, painted by the real Goya. Therefore the screen Alba requires a convincing story line to involve her viewers, rather than the vacuous charade stitched together out of whole cloth and paraded before the cameras like so many of Franciosa's models in the church sequence.

Gardner was in London for an operation on her face to reduce the pressure of the hematoma against her cheek, when she got word that Tyrone Power had died. They hadn't been particularly friendly when filming *The Sun Also Rises*, but she had become closer to him in the past weeks. Power was only nine years older than Gardner and the realization that someone so chronologically near to her could die affected her deeply. She told David Hanna, "You know, this isn't funny. This hits kind of close. He was in our age bracket. I'm worried." For several years, both before and after leaving Metro, she had been concerned about money, about her limitless ability to spend it, or simply squander it, and what she perceived as her diminishing ability to earn it. Pandro S. Berman, the producer of *Bhowani Junction*, had tried to talk to her when they were working on that film: "She was pretty distraught over money—she had been in the business for fourteen years and she had no money to show for it. She had spent every cent. I gave her a lot of advice. I frightened the hell out of her. It was probably the first time in her life that anyone dared to tell her the truth." So her myriad fears coalesced at this point; her terror of losing her looks, of going broke and of dying, and she resolved to get a firmer grip on her finances and her professional life.

Gardner's first step in this direction was to agree to make *On the Beach* (1959) for director Stanley Kramer, a film which would reunite her with Gregory Peck, this time more successfully than in their previous two films. Kramer remembers their first meeting: "I was impressed by how deeply she understood her role—not intellectually, but with a sensitive and humane intuition."

The film depicts the aftermath of

ON THE BEACH (1959).
With Gregory Peck

a nuclear holocaust which has devastated most of the world and left a small knot of survivors, including an American submarine and its commander, Peck, huddled at the Southern end of the globe. Gardner plays Moira Davidson, the wry, hard-drinking woman who falls in love with Peck, although he confuses her with his dead wife, a fact that she accepts, even finding it flattering. "I don't like myself much anyway," she says, describing her own dissolution. Gardner has a number of scenes in which she rues the things she never did, or ironically reviews those she regrets doing. Her performance draws a fine line between pathos and sarcasm, managing to be neither self-pitying, nor too stiff-upper-lip. Gardner's role could easily have slipped into caricature, that of a soap opera creature "who finds love only too late," but with windblown hair and tired circles under her eyes, Gardner is virtually perfect as the woman who accepts gratefully what happiness and satisfaction she can under intolerable circumstances.

When the end is near and the first victims of the nuclear fallout are becoming ill, the men of Peck's crew decide they want to head for home in their sub and end their lives close to their families who have already succumbed. Gardner races to say goodbye to Peck, and as they kiss, their faces are silhouetted against the light glinting off the water. It's a rhapsodically beautiful leave-taking, poignant and yearning. Normally a rather prosaic director, Kramer achieves one other scene of fully realized and lyrical passion. On vacation, Gardner and Peck are trapped with a crowd of lustily drinking fishermen. At night, as Peck lights a fire against the rain, a tenor voice begins to sing "Waltzing Matilda," the theme music which runs through the movie. A male chorus joins the singer as Peck rises to embrace Gardner. As they kiss, the camera circles them in a 360 degree pan, enfolding the couple in their last blissful moments before the end.

Peck is good, if a little too staunch, as the Navy officer who resists the idea of a new romance until it's almost too late. Fred Astaire, as a cynical, fatalistic scientist who bears the burden of explaining the philosophical arguments against the arms race and nuclear proliferation, is too self-mocking, too full of *weltschmerz*, and finally too redundant to be really effective as the film's moralistic message-bearer. (This tendency is one of the few flaws in the otherwise sensitive and sensible script John Paxton extracted from Nevil Shute's novel.)

Gardner is the prostitute/heroine, here disguised as a "cabaret girl," of *The Angel Wore Red* (1960), a murky epic about renegade priests, rescued religious relics, and the Loyalists' anti-clerical views during the Spanish Civil War. At the point where padre Dirk Bogarde reaches a crisis of faith he meets Gardner, who hides him from the Fascists and helps him return the relic with which he's been entrusted to the church's protection.

The cast is excellent, but neither Nunnally Johnson's script nor his direction provides adequate motivation for their behavior. To compound the confusion, the foreign actors have been atrociously dubbed, and Joseph Cotten as a correspondent of obscure motivation, wanders through the action tossing off epigrams and exchanging his eye patch for a succession of glass eyes when he wants to make an impression on the señoritas.

Obviously, those involved were, at least at the beginning, impelled by the best of motives, but somewhere along the line the good intentions were diluted. No longer an anti-religious tract documenting the chaos and horror of warfare as it affects the citizenry, the film degenerates into a series of virtually unrelated vignettes.

Bogarde is very fine. His performance as the tortured, doubting priest whose involvement with

THE SIXTIES: THE SLOPE

"I don't think I'm an actress, I never thought I was."

Gardner offers respite from the war, holds the disparate elements of the movie together. Gardner is most convincing and sympathetic as Soledad, the woman who finds something outside her mundane concerns worth sacrificing her life for. There was more to her role in the original concept of the film and Bogarde's remarks help to clarify what went wrong with the film in general: "It was a magnificent part for Ava. It could have done for her what *Two Women* did for Sophia Loren. She really put her heart into it. I think she was anxious to be more selective and make better pictures. She played it without make-up, without a bra, with holes torn in her dress. Then the word came from Hollywood. They wanted more glamour. They put a corset on her and tidied her up. The life went out of Ava after that."

55 Days at Peking (1963) was director Nicholas Ray's last film to date. It almost put producer Samuel Bronston out of business because of its enormous costs, even though it was made more cheaply in Spain than it could have been in the United States. Though the movie

THE ANGEL WORE RED (1960). With Joseph Cotten

has an expensive look, the plot which provided the excuse for the filmic hoopla is thin to the point of emaciation, even if grounded (none too firmly) in fact. The Boxer Rebellion of 1900 is the colorful canvas against which Philip Yordan (thousands of miles and many cinematic leagues from his *Whistle Stop*) has splashed the cartoon events and cardboard figures of his film. According to history, those events unfolded in less than two months, not in the attenuated fifty-five days of the title.

Gardner plays an impoverished, widowed Russian baroness who takes up with Marine Major Charlton Heston in order to keep her hotel room. Her presence in Peking is a slap in the face to her brother-in-law, Kurt Kasznar, not only because he lusts for her, but because she has had an affair with a Chinese general (Leo Genn) and is *persona non grata* with the diplomatic community. When the mutiny starts, Gardner becomes a nurse, helping doctor Paul Lukas with the Allied wounded and pawning her jewelry to buy drugs. This expedition costs her her life; she's wounded and as Lukas probes for the infection which is killing her Gardner gazes up at him and intones, "You won't find it with a knife, Doctor." When Lukas protests that she must live, she sighs, "I *have* lived." Eventually, reinforcements arrive and the rebellion

106

is crushed. *55 Days at Peking* is a soap opera intercut with labyrinthine Oriental politics and burly military heroics.

Heston has the best role and is on screen almost all the time, performing endless feats of heroism and barking appropriately martial commands at every opportunity. He's slightly less successful mouthing double-entendres at Gardner. "I've been in tight places before," he remarks when she comments that their room is small for two people; or when telling her that he's not sleepy, but "ready to turn in, perhaps." Gardner is good with the slim material she has to work with, even when Yordan has her complain of the deteriorating situation inside the walled city: "Mad Americans inside, mad Boxers outside, and mad Russians all over the place." But any film which allows her to change her clothes with each new scene, in spite of a war, can make no claim to versimilitude.

In *Seven Days in May* (1964) Gardner has an extended cameo as Eleanor Holbrook, the former mistress of Burt Lancaster who plays an Air Force general heading a military plot to take over the government in protest against a nuclear disarmament pact with Russia. Kirk Douglas, Lancaster's aide, calls on the lovelorn lady, who is still, as she says, "vulnerable" following her break with Lancaster. Douglas discovers she's kept Lan-

THE ANGEL WORE RED (1960). With Dirk Bogarde

55 DAYS AT PEKING (1963). With Charlton Heston

caster's letters and swipes them, planning to make use of them to compromise Lancaster, if necessary. In spite of her developing affection for Douglas, Gardner angrily throws him out, thinking Lancaster sent him to collect the letters. In vilifying Douglas, she compares him to herself, a woman who "let an Air Force general use her like his personal airplane," then slams the door on him.

When the letters are not used against Lancaster, Douglas returns them to Gardner, and there is a tentative effort by both to repair their friendship. Gardner does a fine job as the somewhat used, self-denigrating woman whose cynicism masks the fact that she still cares for the cold, calculating general with whom she carried on a lengthy, back-street affair. Cautious, drinking too much, Gardner is warm but superficially tough, trying to mend her life yet leave herself open to new and possibly healing alliances.

The Night of the Iguana (1964) is Gardner's best film of the sixties and the last role in which she was used with anything like her maximum starpower. In *Iguana*, three middle-aged people who have reached a turning point in their lives are tossed in with one ancient, some spinster tourists and a predatory blonde at a ramshackle hotel on the Mexican coast. Like the captured iguana on the patio, Richard Burton is "one of God's creatures at the end of his rope." As the Rev. T. Laurence Shannon, he brings the females in his charge to Gardner's Hotel Costa Verde, stranding them while he replenishes his "emotional bank balance." Burton is spooked, played-out, his nerves as frazzled as the clerical collar he can't get around his neck. Deborah Kerr plays a penniless sketch artist who arrives with her poet grandfather (Cyril Delevanti), hoping they can draw and recite in exchange for lodging. Gardner is Maxine Faulk, who knows and understands Burton as well as she understands herself and the biological urges which compel her to keep two beach boys handy for midnight swims. "Even I know the difference between lovin' somebody and just goin' to bed with 'em," she tells Kerr.

Gardner, earthy, blowsy and barefoot throughout, frolics in the water with her studs, then pushes them away in disgust while Burton and Kerr carol their litany of past woes on the patio. Delevanti speaks the poem that he has come to the sea, "the cradle of life," to finish and, having found peace, dies. But the poem has unsettled Gardner who repeats the last line, "the frightened heart of me," in an anxious, troubled whisper. Burton frees the tethered iguana, the symbol of

55 DAYS AT PEKING (1963). With Charlton Heston

their feelings of frantic helplessness, indicating that they may individually or collectively achieve a newfound tranquility.

Gardner, however, declaring that she's "fed up to the teeth and the gums and the jawbone," asks Kerr and Burton to run the hotel while she escapes to El Paso, but Kerr declines graciously and leaves. Burton elects to remain and when Gardner suggests they take a swim in the ocean Burton says that he can get down the hill, but he's not sure he can get back up again—a metaphor for his ability to persevere. Gardner touchingly tells him, "I'll get you back up, baby. I'll always get you back up," and the film closes on their faces as she regards him reassuringly.

Maxine Faulk is one of Williams' archetypal women survivors, like Andrea del Lago in *Sweet Bird of Youth* or Maggie in *Cat on a Hot Tin Roof*—strong, hopeful and desperate. Gardner plays her as a sexy earth mother, raucous, cackling and gloriously vital but with an undercurrent of terror. She's more vulnerable than she admits but she has an indomitable self-awareness and a no-nonsense honesty about life. It's one of Gardner's very best performances, perhaps because once the part was softened and toned down from the harsher role Bette Davis played on stage, Maxine is so like Gardner herself. As one would

have wished to see a thirty-year-old Ava Gardner play Fitzgerald's destructive heroines, one speculates that a forty-five-year-old Gardner would have made a glorious Martha in Edward Albee's *Who's Afraid of Virginia Woolf?*

Gardner learned to trust John Huston when making *Iguana*; as a gag, the grizzled director gave each member of the cast, and Burton's fiancée, Elizabeth Taylor, a revolver but no bullets, as he expected there would be sufficient fireworks on the set. But the combustible elements failed to explode, and filmmaking problems were limited to the heat, lack of refrigeration and bugs. Gardner reported that "I was determined to do my best in the film. I even made myself look awful. I had lines penciled under my eyes, because it was that kind of film."

The Bible (1966) comprises only the first twenty-two chapters of Genesis. Like its source, the film is an episodic work which includes the Creation, Adam and Eve in the Garden of Eden, the Tower of Babel, Noah and the Ark and the story of Abraham and Sarah. George C. Scott, as Abraham, is an impressive, God-fearing patriarch and Gardner is his barren but desirable wife Sarah. Three angels, all played by Peter O'Toole, appear to Abraham and prophesy that Sarah will bear a son and though she has

SEVEN DAYS IN MAY (1964). With Kirk Douglas

SEVEN DAYS IN MAY (1964). With Kirk Douglas

grown old, her hair streaked with grey, in due course Sarah gives birth to Isaac. But, as envisioned by scenarist Christopher Fry and directed by John Huston, Gardner's Sarah is a far cry from the ninety-year-old woman, "a mother of nations," in the Bible's words, who conceives by the intervention of God, just as Scott, although heavily aged with make-up is hardly the ninety-nine-year-old leader of the Canaanites. Gardner is, however, believable as the woman who, lying in their tent with the infant in her arms, asks, "Who would have said unto Abraham, that Sarah should give children suck, for I have borne him a son in his old age."

Gardner is good in her small part, warm, fond and despairing when she realizes she can't satisfy her husband's dearest wish—that she provide him with a male heir. The characters all speak a pseudo-

Biblical prose, which is apt in its context but nevertheless jarring to the ear. Huston, who plays Noah, narrates as the voice of God in stentorian style, and directs with suitable respect for the majesty of his subject.

Just as the sheer size of the Panavision frame overwhelmed the individual stories contained within *55 Days at Peking*, so *The Bible* is ultimately the triumph of special effects and the wide screen over what seem to be the trivial dramas of a few prehistoric types wandering among a variety of landscaped backgrounds. The famous photographer Ernest Haas was commissioned to spend eighteen months preparing and shooting the ten-minute Creation which opens the film, and nothing was spared to make it as spectacular as modern art direction and cinematography were capable of. It's as though both Fry and Huston thought of God as the ultimate art director and made their film as they thought He would want—to the exclusion of all but the most important personal details.

It was during the making of *The Bible* that Gardner had the most recent of her headline-making romances—with her co-star George C. Scott. According to Fred Sidewater, producer Dino de Laurentiis's assistant on the film: "He was hopelessly in love with her and she was not in love with him." The press chronicled the relationship with glee—the fights, the broken crockery, Scott pursuing Gardner back to the United States until finally he desisted and left her alone.

When *The Bible* opened in New York, Gardner gave Rex Reed an interview which was almost as highly publicized as her friendship with Scott. In it she speaks freely about her life style and her career. She announced she was leaving Spain ". . . because I hate Franco and I hate Communists." And she reiterated her oft-expressed contempt for her work: "I hated it. I mean, I'm not exactly stupid or without feeling, and they tried to sell me like a prize hog. The only time I'm happy is when I'm doing absolutely nothing. When I work I vomit all the time. I know nothing about acting so I have one rule—trust the director and give him heart and soul. What I really want to do is get married again. How great it must be to tromp around barefoot and cook for someone who loves you the rest of your life. I've never had a good man.

"I have a mind, but I never got a chance to use it doing (those) lousy pictures Metro turned out. I *feel* a lot, though. God, I'm sorry I wasted those twenty-five years. But I never brought anything to this

NIGHT OF THE IGUANA (1964). As Maxine Faulk

NIGHT OF THE IGUANA (1964). With Richard Burton

NIGHT OF THE IGUANA (1964). With Richard Burton

business and I have no respect for acting. I never did anything to be proud of. After twenty-five years in this business, if all you've got to show for it is *Mogambo* and *The Hucksters* you might as well give up. I never cared much about myself. I didn't have the emotional makeup for acting and I hate exhibitionists anyway. And who the hell was there to help me or teach me acting was anything else?"

These are far from being the words of a woman divided against

herself over her attitude toward either home or career. Yet one remembers the words of Ann Straus from Gardner's early days at Metro: "Her drive was extraordinary and ruthless." And David Hanna, who was present when *The Naked Maja* underwent pre-production agonies, also recalls an Ava Gardner concerned with the filmmaking process: "Like it or not, she was running the show. The producers realized that Ava's objections to the various versions were

THE BIBLE (1966). As Sarah

THE BIBLE (1966). As Sarah

MAYERLING (1969). With Omar Sharif

MAYERLING (1969). With James Mason and Andrea Parisy

valid and ... they turned to her. Against all her usual instincts, Ava was working in the production department. She helped with the rewriting." It was largely due to her patience and perseverance that the film, whether or not it emerged as a masterpiece, was made at all. Other directors observed her ability to dissect a script with great acumen, to point out its strengths and weaknesses and make suggestions about how a film could be improved.

It is evident that somewhere along the line Gardner made the decision, conscious or not, that since she was always treated like MGM's uncared-for stepchild, she had better look out for her own interests. Many of her career decisions when she was on her own indicate that she didn't necessarily know what was best for her, but in the absence of better roles who could blame her for doing *Mayerling* (1969) of *The Bluebird* (1976)? And as her options were narrowed by

121

MAYERLING (1969). With Omar Sharif

approaching middle-age, she is one of the few female stars who has managed to keep herself constantly employed. Where other stars like Olivia de Havilland, Joan Crawford or Loretta Young were constrained by their images of themselves, by fear of facing the cameras, or by the lack of suitable roles, Gardner has played cameos (*The Life and Times of Judge Roy Bean*, 1972), roles for which she received star billing but did not have a starring role (*The Cassandra Crossing*, (1977) and in films beneath her abilities in which she did have the lead (*Tam Lin*, 1971 and *Permission to Kill*, 1975).

Gardner plays the Empress Elizabeth of Austria-Hungary in Terence Young's remake of the 1936 *Mayerling* (1969). The action has been expanded, inflated beyond recognition, to encompass court intrigue, European politics, extremist plots, student insurrections, and the strained relations between father (Emperor Franz Josef, played by James Mason) and son (Prince Rudolf, played by Omar Sharif).

Rudolf was married to the Belgian Princess Stephanie, but never bothered to keep his partying or numerous infidelities a secret until he met Marie Vetsera (Catherine Deneuve). They had a brief, clandestine affair which was regarded with favor by the Empress and fury by the Emperor. In 1888 Marie and Rudolf were found dead, joined in a suicide pact at the royal hunting lodge at Mayerling. Although extremely beautiful, Deneuve seems hardly the sort of girl men kill themselves over or renounce thrones for. Sharif plays Rudolf with his customary anemic charm; the only moments in which his plight is tinged with the tragedy the real lovers suffered are those he shares with Gardner, who understands what he's going through and sympathizes with him in a manner more womanly than maternal.

Sharif is ten years Gardner's junior, so it is hardly typecasting to have him play her son or to make her a grandmother. Since Sharif is totally inept in handling emotionally charged encounters, the burden of making these infrequent meetings between mother and son credible falls to Gardner. She rises gracefully and touchingly to the challenge, portraying Elizabeth as an accomplished and neglected woman who shrinks from her public role but wishes to be closer to her son than their separate lives permit. She appears at a fancy dress ball but retires immediately, saying, "You know I hate being stared at," one of the many autobiographical lines which crop up in Gardner's on-screen dialogue.

The film is plush and pretentious, stodgily directed by Terence Young, but the reviews praised

Gardner's performance in glowing terms. Howard Thompson of *The New York Times* said, "The surprise of the picture is Ava Gardner as the enigmatic Empress of Austria . . . With an uncertain smile and a husky voice, this beautiful lady is the most beguiling character in the movie. She movingly underplays her few scenes."

Pauline Kael noted in her *New Yorker* column that "The choice of Ava Gardner—a star famous for her beauty and underacting—to play Sharif's mother, the empress, seems almost inspired. (She and Mason) are of the same lineage; spawn of the movies, they even resemble each other, and one would have to work hard to dislike either one of them."

Gardner's next picture underwent three title changes before its limited release and almost immediate sale to television. *Tam Lin* (1971) was directed by Gardner's old friend Roddy McDowall, who deplored the recutting that the producer, Commonwealth International, in a state of decline from which it never emerged, imposed upon the film. Nevertheless, the material was hardly auspicious to start with. An old fairy tale, most recently a poem by Robert Burns, it concerned a Queen of the Fairies who trapped young men to keep her youthful. William Spier's screenplay has Gardner mouth axioms like "Life is an illusion. Therefore nothing is permanent," maintain a stable full of studs to cavort around her with a few young women thrown in to keep the numbers even, and threaten her straying inamorata with death by automobile crash when he has notions of departing. She was gorgeously gowned by Balmain in a group of spiky outfits presumably intended to stress her predatory nature, and unflatteringly photographed by Billy Williams.

Gardner next accepted a cameo in John Huston's *The Life and Times of Judge Roy Bean* (1972) which starred Paul Newman as the famous hanging judge who renamed the town of Vinegaroon, Texas after his adored Lily

THE SEVENTIES: PEACE AND QUIET

"I don't lie about my age. What's the point?"

Langtry. The Jersey Lily visits her namesake after the judge's death, although they had been pen pals while he lived. She makes a spectacular entrance swathed in lace and tulle, sweeps around the judge's miserable way station and departs, presumably trailing violet water and lavender in her wake. The epilogue in which she appears is rather pointless; since the film does take liberties with Bean's life story, it would have been more moving if the two had met before his death, rather than showing her in this mysterious non-encounter.*

Earthquake (1974), Universal's symphony in Sensurround, reunited Gardner with Charlton Heston and director Mark Robson (*The Little Hut*), whose wooden style is more appropriate to a film in which the real stars are rumbles on the sound track and the special effects wizardry of Frank Brendel (he won an Academy Award for his not inconsiderable achievements). Sensurround is the Universal trade-

* In William Wyler's 1940 film, *The Westerner*, Walter Brennan as Judge Bean sees his beloved Lily in the flesh just before he dies.

125

TAM LIN (1972). As Michaela Cazaret

mark for low-frequency sound vibrations which cause an actual physical tremor in theatres which installed the equipment to handle it. *Earthquake* is twentieth in *Variety's* list of all-time film rental champions and has made over $36 million but this information does not indicate that it is great art. *Earthquake* is emphatically middle-brow in its aims and realization, providing maximum terror for a minimum of emotional and intellectual effort. It has a cast of one-from-each-category of stereotypes, including Gardner as Remy Graff, the neurotic, pill-popping, suicide-threatening wife of Stewart Graff (Heston), a staunch architectural engineer working for his father-in-law, Lorne Greene, and Genevieve Bujold as the young widow-with-a-son-who-gets-lost-in-the-cataclysm. Bujold is also the woman into whose arms Heston is driven by his shrewish wife's nagging and suspicions. George Kennedy plays a dumb, kind, leather-lunged cop and Marjoe Gortner a would-be rapist who hides his touseled blonde curls under a wig when he reports for duty with the National Guard. These are merely the cardboard figures propped in front of a collapsing dam, a jiggling Richter scale, and some harrassed public functionaries of varying degrees of ineptitude. Gardner has no better and

no worse a time of it than anyone else, and manages to survive the experience, but not the movie, with her dignity intact.

At the end, as Heston strives to help the trapped victims of a second tremor to exit a sealed building, the dam breaks and the water mains become flooded. Gardner is swept away in the rush, and Heston, with Bujold reaching down to him from above, chooses to rescue his wife. The *Village Voice* aptly expressed the rationale behind this decision: ". . . the choice of death with Gardner over life with Bujold works iconographically, because Heston and Gardner belong together as images, if not as characters. . . . both were major stars at about the same time, the last period of studio-groomed movie stars, and both have maintained something of a star quality. Even a slightly puffy 52-year-old Gardner is more interesting to look at than Bujold. Whatever the logic of the plot may demand, an axiom of the cinema like Heston has to belong more to Gardner than Bujold, and in the view of the film the two of them belong together in death. In a nasty juxtaposition of images full of typical Hollywood self-hatred, these last two figures of the old Hollywood are swept down a sewer pipe to certain death."

Pauline Kael, writing in the *New Yorker* with her customary acuity,

THE LIFE AND TIMES OF JUDGE ROY BEAN (1972).
As Lily Langtry

EARTHQUAKE (1974). With Lorne Greene

said, "The treatment of the film's two principal stars, Charlton Heston and Ava Gardner, could almost be the in-joke of an industry that enjoys the idea of self-destructing. Gardner was one of the last women stars to make it on beauty alone. She never looked really happy in her movies; she wasn't quite there, but she never suggested that she was anywhere else, either. She had a dreamy, hurt quality, a generously modelled mouth, and faraway eyes. Maybe what turned people on was that her sensuality was developed but her personality wasn't. She was a rootless, beautiful stray, somehow incomplete but never ordinary, and just about impossible to dislike, since she was utterly without affectation. But to Universal she is just one more old star to beef up a picture's star power, and so she's cast as a tiresome bitch whose husband (Heston) is fed up with her. She looks blowsy and beat-out, and that could be fun if she were allowed to be blowzily good-natured, like the heroine of *Mogambo* twenty years later, but the script here harks back to those old movies in which a husband is justified in leaving his wife only if she was a jealous schemer who made his life hell. Ava Gardner might make a man's life hell out of indolence and spiritual absenteeism, but out of shrill stupidity? *Earthquake*, though, isn't the sort of project in which the

EARTHQUAKE (1974). With Charlton Heston

moviemakers care whether the role fits the performer. They got what they wanted. Ava Gardner's name lifts *Earthquake* out of the Universal-action-picture category."

Thirty-two years after her Hollywood career began, Gardner was finally being paid some serious critical attention; these two reviews are the most extensive critiques of her work she ever received for any film, and for a piece of hack work the Metro Gardner would have screamed bloody murder at rather than appear in. But if Universal got what it wanted, so did Gardner. "To be honest," she told the *Ladies Home Journal*, "I needed a paid vacation. I wasn't paid that much. I was just ready for a change of scenery."

Ultimately, *Earthquake* is earthquack, the Mickey Mouse of disaster films, and, while it isn't blatantly offensive, it does nothing for its stars, its makers, the studio, or the disaster genre; it just squats on the screen registering zero on the Richter scale of motion picture entertainment.

Permission to Kill (1975) has all the earmarks of a tax shelter, but even tax shelters are intended to make money, a compensation denied to the producers of this film. The international cast is headed by Dirk Bogarde as an obscurely motivated British agent who wants Bekim Fehmiu, head of the Communist National Liberation Party and Gardner's ex-lover, to stay in the West rather than "go back," as the script repeatedly expresses his inclination to duck behind the Iron Curtain. Paid assassins, black-mailed homosexuals and co-opted reporters are assembled in Gmunden, Upper Austria to head Fehmiu off, but to no avail. After a number of confrontations—some breathy, some heated, some rous-ing, but none suspenseful or even moderately amusing—Fehmiu is blown to small bits in an airport shootout and explosion which fails to detonate so much as a ripple of interest on screen. Freddie Young's Panavision camera work is the most arresting aspect of this otherwise spiritually and cinematically bankrupt effort, directed with a lack of style by Cyril Frankel. Gardner emotes in a style unsuited to the vehicle in which she finds herself, but this was done, obviously, in the absence of any suggestion to the contrary by Frankel.

Gardner next found *herself* behind the Iron Curtain in the first Russo-American co-production, an adaptation of Maurice Maeter-linck's *The Blue Bird* (1976), directed by George Cukor, an old-time and old-style *metteur en scène* for whom Gardner professed affec-tion from their *Bhowani Junction* days. *The Blue Bird* is a fantasy and to be successful it must be ap-proached with the greatest delicacy

EARTHQUAKE (1974). With Charlton Heston

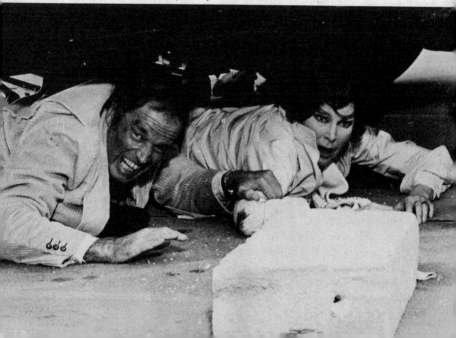

PERMISSION TO KILL (1975). With Frederic Forrest

and restraint. The combined Russian/American onslaught mounted against this defenseless target inundated it with "production values," a "look it's-Robert Morley/Will Geer/Cicely Tyson, etc." cast and a leaden, rather tortured style which is completely self-defeating. There are some particularly unattractive paintings which serve as curtain raisers for each segment of the children's journey in search of the mythical blue bird.

Elizabeth Taylor does very nicely in her quadruple roles and Jane Fonda has fun camping it up as Night. Gardner performs Luxury as a parody of her earlier femme fatale image, appearing swathed in scarlet to sweep the boy (Todd Lookinland) literally off his feet and transport him to her castle where some slue-footed revellers are desporting themselves with sodden abandon. Gardner is perfect as Luxury, full of soft, seductive, throaty laughter and dimpled smiles. Would that the production were as beautiful as her face. But *The Blue Bird* is, for the most part, a charmless, cluttered, literal-minded non-fairy tale.

Gardner has little dialogue and the section in which she appears is brief. Orgies are not for young boys, a factor she takes into account when Lookinland asks what kind of luxury she represents. "You'll find out when you're a little

PERMISSION TO KILL (1975). As Katina Petersen

older," she purrs in 19th century Russia's equivalent of "Come up and see me some time."

The Cassandra Crossing (1977) is an upbeat disaster film complete with rampaging pneumonic plague, a sealed train full of presumably doomed passengers, and a flint-hearted Army colonel (Burt Lancaster) determined to run the train into Poland and dump the hapless travelers off a rickety, isolated span before the story, or the disease, can leak out and create an international panic.

The penumones get loose in Geneva when two Swedish terrorists accidentally shoot up a vat of virulent bacteria during the course of a raid on the International Health Organization. One carries it onto the train and most of the passengers quickly become infected. Richard Harris and Sophia Loren play a divorced couple, a doctor and a writer respectively, who meet on the train and supervise the rest of the riders. Gardner, as Nicole (Mrs. Hugo Dressler) is travelling with her dog and her gigolo, Martin Sheen, who uses her customs priorities to smuggle heroin across various borders.

Gardner wisecracks her way through the calamity, remarking, "Heroin. How common, darling," when Sheen's racket is discovered, and swiping food for her pet from her fellow passenger's plates. She

tells an armed medical team which boards the train, "You know that my Hugo makes these," indicating their guns. "He'll be so pleased you're using them." Garnder has a costume change for every occasion, turning up in fur to board the train, black for meditation, and a simple blouse and skirt for the nastier skirmishes. While her lover is climbing around the outside of the sealed car and Harris is blowing holes in propane gas tanks in their efforts to escape the train, she's whisking into a new outfit.

The Cassandra Crossing (the title refers to the bridge, which was so dangerous the natives fled for fear it would collapse upon them) is composed of fragments collected, tongue in cheek, from *The Andromeda Strain*, *The Lady Vanishes*, *Voyage of the Damned*, and *Panic in the Streets*. It is an interesting example of an overworked subject taking on new life through the use of satire, humor and a cheerful disregard for probability or logic, and by exploiting the actors' previous screen incarnations as the basis for their present roles: Harris's role is derived from his straight bomb expert aboard the *Juggernaut*; Loren is competent and energetic à la *Arabesque*; and Gardner is an aging barefoot contessa, reduced to paying for sex, but doing so with style. The characters are clichéd

THE BLUE BIRD (1976). With Todd Lookinland

THE BLUE BIRD (1976). As Luxury

THE CASSANDRA CROSSING (1977). As Nicole

*THE CASSANDRA CROSSING (1977). With Richard Harris,
Sophia Loren, and Martin Sheen*

and the film isn't great art, but *The
Cassandra Crossing* is fast-moving
and involving, and the aerial
photography (by George Pan
Cosmatos who also directed) is
spectacular.

Gardner had six days of work
(but her name above the title, albeit
in sixth place) in a truly small
cameo for Universal's *The Sentinel*
(1977). She plays Miss Logan, a
serene and enigmatic real estate
agent who, at first, informs heroine

Cristina Raines that an apartment
is $500 a month, then quickly
lowers the rent when Raines balks.
Her reason gradually becomes clear
after Raines has a number of
horrifying experiences alone in the
dead of night. Eventually, it
develops that Raines, as a resident
of this particular building, has been
chosen as the Sentinel, who guards
the entrance to hell and protects the
Earth from the powers of evil. Before she can be installed, however,

THE SENTINEL (1977). As Miss Logan

THE SENTINEL (1977). With Cristina Raines

she must commit suicide; the film details several attempts to drive her mad and persuade her to take her own life.

The building is demolished, but the site is evidently under the same curse, for at the end Raines is seen from a distance, seated in a window; she has become the Sentinel. Gardner, still in the business of recruiting young blood for the minions of hell, shows a couple to an apartment and casually remarks when they notice the figure upstairs, "She's a recluse. She's no problem at all. She's a nun."

The screenplay is completely delirious, full of giddy dialogue and opportunities for plummy overacting, especially by Burgess Meredith, who pops around Raines' building with a canary and a cat, and invites Raines to a birthday party for the cat, with "a black and white cake for a black and white cat." Meredith is delightful as Raines' fey neighbor, especially in comparison with Raines and Chris Sarandon (as her boyfriend), who are boringly inexpressive. Michael Winner, presumably hoping to duplicate the success of *The*

Exorcist, directed in a gross and oversimplified manner which leaves nothing to the imagination. With his co-scriptwriter (and the author of the book), Jeffrey Konvitz, he assaults the intellect during the first 4/5 of the film; for the latter 1/5 he assails the senses with a disgusting parade of putrifying demons who try to lure Raines into hell. As a horror film, *The Sentinel* is a disgrace—derivative, banal and nauseating, and it's unfortunate that Gardner agreed to appear in it.

Gardner has little to do but act smooth, sarcastic and exasperated when Raines wants her to show her through the building, looking for unwelcome nocturnal visitors. Her part is far from terrifying; in fact all of her scenes take place in bright sunlight as if to contradict the reality of her sinister profession. Gardner exudes old-time Hollywood glamour, a welcome relief from the stolid stylelessness of many of her fellow performers.

If acting is an art, no movie star leads a more "artless" life than Ava Gardner. She is neither some mysterious, legendary "other" inhabiting a nether world composed in the fantasies of her idolators, à la Garbo, nor an all too flesh and blood creature like Elizabeth Taylor, relentlessly marrying and divorcing on America's front pages. Nor is Gardner a figure inhabiting the middle ground where reality and dreams are supposed to meet. She is now a quiet, almost withdrawn person who shuns all attempts to invade her privacy. She has reached the age where her personal life is, at long last, her own business; flashbulbs no longer give her nightmares. She is still beautiful, still working steadily (mostly in roles that are glorified cameos) and she is still a star who gets star billing no matter how small her part.

Gone are the days when the United Elevator Operators would vote her "The girl they would like to be stuck with at the top of the Empire State Building," or Cole Porter would write, in his song "Stereophonic Sound," from his fifties musical, *Silk Stockings*, "If Ava Gardner played Godiva riding on a mare/The people wouldn't pay a cent to see her in the bare/Unless she had glorious Technicolor . . . /or Stereophonic Sound."

Gardner has managed to survive a lifetime spent in an industry

LONDON

"If I were really as sad and lonely as some of the stories say, I'd blow my brains out."

where there are few survivors, only a long line of the walking wounded, and she has done it on her own terms. She set out her credo early in her career when she was criticized for the way she conducted her life: "I'll go on living according to my own standards." And she has been true to her word.

It's arguable whether or not Gardner, as she claimed, made better films when MGM loaned her out or later as an independent when she had charge of her own career. After all, *Show Boat*, *Pandora and the Flying Dutchman*, *Mogambo* and *Bhowani Junction* were made at her home studio and they show a commendable willingness on Metro's part to allow not only a change of pace but maturity and complexity to play an increasingly important part in her on-screen development. The healthy young Gardner of her early lesser vehicles evolves into the heartsick, conscience-wracked heroine of *Bhowani Junction*, and if both films are dependent on her image as a movie queen, it scarcely matters. If not to be a movie queen, why was "Avah Gadnuh" plucked from

Larry Tarr's photography studio and turned, Cinderella style, into a goddess?

Although Gardner has consistently derided her lack of an education, anybody who could count Robert Graves and Ernest Hemingway among her friends emphatically has more to offer than her looks. Gardner has always hidden behind a pose of indifference about her career and of not working at her roles. But the comments of her directors (Stanley Kramer, for example) and co-workers and her own biting accuracy in evaluating her parts indicate that she has expended a great deal more thought and effort on her occupation than she is willing to take credit for. Her reticence in taking responsibility for and guiding her work is a curious facet of her personality. On one hand, Gardner blames MGM for neglecting her career and anguishes over what she could have done if the studio had cared, but in the same breath, she declares, "I've failed at the only things I really have wanted, a husband and children," casually ignoring thirty-five years of her life.

The Ava Gardner of 1977 has found tranquility in London, in the company of her secretary, Betty Kean, and her pet Corgi, and without a man. She retains a touching fondness for her ex-husbands: "All three of my husbands were extraordinary men. Each was a genius. I have happy memories of each of them. I don't regret my marriages for a moment." And she avoids the clamor of the fans. "It's lovely to have people recognize me in the street. They may not know my name, but my face is familiar to them and they smile and nod their heads. That's sweet."

If the exotic appeal and the lush sensuality which transfixed moviegoers in the fifties exist today predominantly in the memories of her beholders, it doesn't seem to matter. What counts is that she's *there* on the screen, in triumph or in trash, purring huskily, snapping her green eyes and defying the world not to like her. As she says, "I'm one Hollywood star who hasn't tried to slash her wrists, take sleeping pills, or kick a cop in the shins." Attagirl, Ava!

BIBLIOGRAPHY

Fordin, Hugh. *The World of Entertainment*. New York: Doubleday and Co., 1973.

Gussow, Mel. *Don't Say Yes Until I Finish Talking*. New York: Doubleday and Co., 1971.

Hanna, David. *Ava, a Portrait of a Star*. New York: G.P. Putnam's Sons, 1960.

Higham, Charles. *Ava, A Life Story*. New York: Dell Publishing Co., 1974.

Hotchner, A.E. *Papa Hemingway*. New York: Random House, 1966.

Hyams, Joe. *Bogie: The Biography of Humphrey Bogart*. New York: The New American Library, 1966.

Parish, James Robert and Ronald L. Bowers. *The MGM Stock Company*. New Rochelle, New York: Arlington House, 1973.

Reed, Rex. *Do You Sleep in the Nude?* New York: The New American Library, 1968.

Shipman, David. *The Great Movie Stars, The International Years*. Great Britain: St. Martins Press, 1972.

THE FILMS OF AVA GARDNER

The director's name follows the release date. A (c) following the release date in-dicates that the film was in color. Sp indicates screenplay and b/o indicates based/on.

1. WE WERE DANCING. MGM, 1942. *Robert Z. Leonard*. Sp: Claudine West, Hans Rameau and George Froeschel, b/o play by Noël Coward from a group of plays presented as *Tonight at 8:30*. Cast: Norma Shearer, Melvyn Douglas, Gail Patrick, Lee Bowman, Florence Bates.

2. JOE SMITH, AMERICAN. MGM, 1942. *Richard Thorpe*. Sp: Allen Rivkin, b/o story by Paul Gallico. Cast: Robert Young, Marsha Hunt, Darryl Hickman, Harvey Stephens.

3. SUNDAY PUNCH. MGM, 1942. *David Miller*. Sp: Fay and Michael Kanin and Allen Rivkin. Cast: William Lundigan, Jean Rogers, Dan Dailey, Guy Kibbee, Sam Levene, J. Carrol Naish.

4. THIS TIME FOR KEEPS. MGM, 1942. *Charles Reisner*. Sp: Muriel Roy Bolton, Rian James and Harry Ruskin, b/o characters created by Herman J. Mankiewicz. Cast: Ann Rutherford, Robert Sterling, Guy Kibbee, Irene Rich.

5. CALLING DR. GILLESPIE. MGM, 1942. *Harold Bucquet*. Sp: Willis Goldbeck and Harry Ruskin, b/o story by Kubec Glasmon and characters created by Max Brand. Cast: Lionel Barrymore, Philip Dorn, Donna Reed, Nat Pendleton, Alma Kruger.

6. KID GLOVE KILLER. MGM, 1942. *Fred Zinnemann*. Sp: Allen Rivkin and John C. Higgins. Cast: Van Heflin, Marsha Hunt, Lee Bowman, Samuel S. Hinds, John Litel. *Eddie Quillan, CATHERINE LEWIS*

B/o STORY by HIGGINS

7. REUNION IN FRANCE. MGM, 1942. *Jules Dassin*. Sp: Jan Lustig, Marvin Borowsky and Marc Connelly, b/o story by Ladislaus Bus-Fekete. Cast: John Wayne, Joan Crawford, Philip Dorn, Reginald Owen, Albert Basserman, John Carradine, Henry Daniell.

8.   PILOT NO. 5. MGM, 1943. *George Sidney*. Sp: David Hertz. Cast: Gene
Kelly, Franchot Tone, Marsha Hunt, Van Johnson, Alan Baxter.

9.   GHOSTS ON THE LOOSE. Monogram, 1943. *William Beaudine*. Sp:
Kenneth Higgins. Cast: Bela Lugosi, Leo Gorcey, Huntz Hall, Bobby Jordan,
Minerva Urecal, Stanley Clements, Ric Vallin.

10.   LOST ANGEL. MGM, 1943. *Roy Rowland*. Sp: Isobel Lennart, b/o idea
by Angna Enters. Cast: Margaret O'Brien, James Craig, Marsha Hunt, Philip
Merivale.

11.   HITLER'S MADMAN. MGM, 1943. *Douglas Sirk*. Sp: Peretz Hirshbein,
Melvin Levy and Doris Malloy, b/o story by Emil Ludwig and Albrecht Joseph
and *Hangman's Village* by Bart Lytton. Cast: Patricia Morison, John Carradine,
Alan Curtis, Ralph Morgan., EDGAR KENNEDY, JIMMY CONLIN

12.   SWING FEVER. MGM, 1944. *Tim Whelan*. Sp: Nat Perrin and Warren
Wilson, b/o story by Matt Brooks and Joseph Hoffman. Cast: Kay Kyser,
Marilyn Maxwell, William Gargan, Nat Pendleton, Curt Bois.

13.   THREE MEN IN WHITE. MGM, 1944. *Willis Goldbeck*. Sp: Martin
Berkeley and Harry Ruskin, b/o characters created by Max Brand. Cast: Van
Johnson, Lionel Barrymore, Marilyn Maxwell, Keye Luke.

14.   BLONDE FEVER. MGM, 1944. *Richard Whorf*. Sp: Patricia Coleman,
b/o play by Ferenc Molnar. Cast: Philip Dorn, Mary Astor, Felix Bressart, Gloria
Grahame, Marshall Thompson.

15.   MAISIE GOES TO RENO. MGM, 1944. *Harry Beaumont*. Sp: Mary C.
McCall, Jr., b/o story by Harry Ruby and James O'Hanlon. Cast: Ann Sothern,
John Hodiak, Tom Drake, Paul Cavanagh, MARTA LINDEN, DONALD MEEK

16.   TWO GIRLS AND A SAILOR. MGM, 1944. *Richard Thorpe*. Sp: Richard
Connell and Gladys Lehman. Cast: June Allyson, Van Johnson, Jose Iturbi, Gloria
DeHaven, Jimmy Durante, Tom Drake, Lena Horne.

17.   SHE WENT TO THE RACES. MGM, 1945. *Willis Goldbeck*. Sp:
Lawrence Hazard, b/o story by Alan Friedman and De Vallon Scott. Cast: James

Craig, Frances Gifford, Edmund Gwenn, Sig Ruman, Reginald Owen, J.M. Kerrigan.

18. WHISTLE STOP. United Artists, 1946. *Leonide Moguy*. Sp: Philip Yordan, b/o novel by Maritta M. Wolff. Cast: George Raft, Tom Conway, Victor McLaglen, Jorja Cartwright, Florence Bates.

19. THE KILLERS. Universal, 1946. *Robert Siodmak*. Sp: Anthony Veiller, b/o short story by Ernest Hemingway. Cast: Burt Lancaster, Edmond O'Brien, Albert Dekker, Sam Levene, Jack Lambert, Jeff Corey, Donald McBride, William Conrad, Charles McGraw, Vince Barnett. Remade in 1964.

20. THE HUCKSTERS. MGM, 1947. *Jack Conway*. Sp: Luther Davis, b/o adaptation by Edward Chodorov and George Wells of novel by Frederic Wakeman. Cast: Clark Gable, Deborah Kerr, Edward Arnold, Sydney Greenstreet, Adolphe Menjou, Keenan Wynn.

21. SINGAPORE. Universal, 1947. *John Brahm*. Sp: Seton I. Miller and Robert Thoeren, b/o story by Seton I. Miller. Cast: Fred MacMurray, Roland Culver, Richard Haydn, Spring Byington, Thomas Gomez, Porter Hall.

22. ONE TOUCH OF VENUS. Universal, 1948. *William A. Seiter*. Sp: Harry Kurnitz and Frank Tashlin, b/o *The Tinted Venus* by F. Anstey and the play by S. J. Perelman and Ogden Nash, with music by Kurt Weill. Cast: Robert Walker, Eve Arden, Dick Haymes, Olga San Juan, Tom Conway.

23. THE GREAT SINNER. MGM, 1949. *Robert Siodmak*. Sp: Christopher Isherwood and Ladislas Fodor, b/o the Ladislas Fodor and Rene Fueleop-Miller adaptation of Feodor Dostoievsky's *The Gambler*. Cast: Gregory Peck, Melvyn Douglas, Frank Morgan, Agnes Moorehead, Walter Huston, Ethel Barrymore.

24. EAST SIDE, WEST SIDE. MGM, 1949. *Mervyn LeRoy*. Sp: Isobel Lennart, b/o novel by Marcia Davenport. Cast: James Mason, Barbara Stanwyck, Van Heflin, Cyd Charisse, Nancy Davis, Gale Sondergaard, William Conrad, Beverly Michaels, WM. FRAWLEY, DOUGLAS KENNEDY

25. THE BRIBE. MGM, 1949. *Robert Z. Leonard*. Sp: Marguerite Roberts, b/o short story by Frederick Nebel. Cast: Robert Taylor, Charles Laughton, Vincent Price, John Hodiak., John Hoyt, Samuel S. Hinds MARTIN GALLARAGA

150

26. MY FORBIDDEN PAST. RKO, 1951. *Robert Stevenson*. Sp: Marion Parsonnet, Leopold Atlas, b/o *Carriage Entrance* by Polan Banks. Cast: Robert Mitchum, Melvyn Douglas, Janis Carter, Lucile Watson, Basil Ruysdael, Gordon Oliver.

27. SHOW BOAT. MGM, 1951 (c). *George Sidney*. Sp: John Lee Mahin, b/o novel by Edna Ferber and play by Oscar Hammerstein II, with music by Jerome Kern. Cast: Kathryn Grayson, Howard Keel, Joe E. Brown, Marge and Gower Champion, Robert Sterling, Agnes Moorehead, William Warfield. Remake of 1929 and 1936 films.

28. PANDORA AND THE FLYING DUTCHMAN. MGM, 1951 (c). *Albert Lewin*. Sp: Albert Lewin, b/o legend of the Flying Dutchman. Cast: James Mason, Nigel Patrick, Sheila Sim, Marius Goring, Mario Cabre, Pamela Kellino, Harold Warrender.

29. LONE STAR. MGM, 1952. *Vincent Sherman*. Sp: Borden Chase and Howard Estabrook, b/o story by Borden Chase. Cast: Clark Gable, Broderick Crawford, Lionel Barrymore, Beulah Bondi, Ed Begley. Wm. Conrad

30. SNOWS OF KILIMANJARO. 20th Century-Fox, 1952 (c). *Henry King*. Sp: Casey Robinson, b/o story by Ernest Hemingway. Cast: Gregory Peck, Susan Hayward, Hildegarde Neff, Leo G. Carroll, Marcel Dalio.

31. RIDE, VAQUERO! MGM, 1953 (c). *John Farrow*. Sp: Frank Fenton. Cast: Robert Taylor, Howard Keel, Anthony Quinn, Kurt Kasznar, Ted de Corsia.

32. MOGAMBO. MGM, 1953 (c). *John Ford*. Sp: John Lee Mahin, b/o play by Wilson Collison. Cast: Clark Gable, Grace Kelly, Donald Sinden, Philip Stainton, Eric Pohlman. Remake of *Red Dust*, 1932.

33. KNIGHTS OF THE ROUND TABLE. MGM, 1953 (c). *Richard Thorpe*. Sp: Talbot Jennings, Jan Lustig and Noel Langley, b/o *Le Morte D'Arthur* by Sir Thomas Malory. Cast: Robert Taylor, Mel Ferrer, Anne Crawford, Stanley Baker, Felix Aylmer.

34. THE BAREFOOT CONTESSA. United Artists, 1954 (c). *Joseph L. Mankiewicz*. Sp: Joseph L. Mankiewicz. Cast: Humphrey Bogart, Edmond O'Brien, Marius Goring, Valentina Cortesa, Rossano Brazzi, Elizabeth Sellars, Warren Stevens, Bessie Love.

35. BHOWANI JUNCTION. MGM, 1956 (c). *George Cukor*. Sp: Sonya Levien and Ivan Moffat, b/o novel by John Masters. Cast: Stewart Granger, Bill Travers, Abraham Sofaer, Lionel Jeffries, Francis Matthews.

36. THE LITTLE HUT. MGM, 1957 (c). *Mark Robson*. Sp: F. Hugh Herbert, b/o play by Andre Roussin, English adaptation by Nancy Mitford. Cast: Stewart Granger, David Niven, Walter Chiari, Finlay Currie.

37. THE SUN ALSO RISES. 20th Century-Fox, 1957 (c). *Henry King*. Sp: Peter Viertel, b/o novel by Ernest Hemingway. Cast: Tyrone Power, Errol Flynn, Eddie Albert, Mel Ferrer, Juliette Greco, Robert Evans, Marcel Dalio, Henry Daniell. GREGORY RATOFF

38. THE NAKED MAJA. United Artists, 1959 (c). *Henry Koster*. Sp: Norman Corwin and Giorgio Prosperi, b/o story by Oscar Saul and Talbot Jennings. Cast: Anthony Franciosa, Amedeo Nazzari, Gino Cervi, Lea Padovani, Massimo Serato.

39. ON THE BEACH. A Stanley Kramer Production, released by United Artists, 1959. *Stanley Kramer*. Sp: John Paxton, b/o novel by Nevil Shute. Cast: Gregory Peck, Fred Astaire, Anthony Perkins, Donna Anderson, Guy Doleman.

40. THE ANGEL WORE RED. MGM, 1960. *Nunnally Johnson*. Sp: Nunnally Johnson. Cast: Dirk Bogarde, Joseph Cotten, Vittorio de Sica, Aldo Fabrizi, Finlay Currie.

41. 55 DAYS AT PEKING. Allied Artists, 1963 (c). *Nicholas Ray*. Sp: Philip Yordan and Bernard Gordon. Cast: Charlton Heston, David Niven, Flora Robson, Robert Helpmann, John Ireland, Paul Lukas, Leo Genn, Elizabeth Sellars.

42. SEVEN DAYS IN MAY. Paramount, 1964. *John Frankenheimer*. Sp: Rod Serling, b/o novel by Fletcher Knebel and Charles W. Bailey II. Cast: Kirk Douglas, Burt Lancaster, Fredric March, Edmond O'Brien, Martin Balsam, George Macready, Whit Bissell, Hugh Marlowe, John Houseman, Richard Anderson.

43. THE NIGHT OF THE IGUANA. MGM, 1964. *John Huston*. Sp: Anthony Veiller and John Huston, b/o play by Tennessee Williams. Cast: Richard Burton, Deborah Kerr, Sue Lyon, Grayson Hall, Skip Ward, Cyril Delevanti.

44.   THE BIBLE. 20th Century-Fox, 1966 (c). *John Huston*. Sp: Christopher
Fry. Cast: George C. Scott, Richard Harris, Michael Parks, Stephen Boyd, Peter
O'Toole, Franco Nero, Ulla Bergryd.

45.   MAYERLING. MGM, 1969 (c). *Terence Young*. Sp: Terence Young and
James Goldman, b/o *Idyl's End* by Claude Anet and *The Archduke* by Michael
Arnold. Cast: James Mason, Catherine Deneuve, Omar Sharif, James Robertson-
Justice, Genevieve Page. Remake of 1936 film.

46.   TAM LIN. AIP, 1971 (c). *Roddy McDowall*. Sp: William Spier. Cast: Ian
McShane, Stephanie Beacham, Cyril Cusack, Richard Wattis, David Whitman,
Madeline Smith, Sinead Cusack.

47.   THE LIFE AND TIMES OF JUDGE ROY BEAN. National General,
1972 (c). *John Huston*. Sp: John Milius. Cast: Paul Newman, Jacqueline Bisset,
Tab Hunter, John Huston, Stacy Keach, Anthony Perkins, Roddy McDowall,
Victoria Principal, Anthony Zerbe.

48.   EARTHQUAKE. Universal, 1974 (c). *Mark Robson*. Sp: George Fox and
Mario Puzo. Cast: Charlton Heston, George Kennedy, Genevieve Bujold, Richard
Roundtree, Marjoe Gortner, Gabriel Dell. LLOYD NOLAN, LORNE GREEN

49.   PERMISSION TO KILL. Avco Embassy, 1975 (c). *Cyril Frankel*. Sp:
Robin Estridge, b/o novel by Robin Estridge. Cast: Dirk Bogarde, Bekim Fehmiu,
Timothy Dalton, Nicole Calfan, Frederic Forrest.

50.   THE BLUE BIRD. 20th Century-Fox, 1976 (c). *George Cukor*. Sp: Hugh
Whitemore and Alfred Hayes, b/o story by Maurice Maeterlinck. Cast: Elizabeth
Taylor, Jane Fonda, Cicely Tyson, Robert Morley, Harry Andrews, Will Geer.

51.   THE CASSANDRA CROSSING. Avco Embassy, 1977 (c). *George Pan
Cosmatos*. Sp: Tom Mankiewicz, Robert Katz and George Pan Cosmatos. Cast:
Sophia Loren, Richard Harris, Burt Lancaster, Ingrid Thulin, Martin Sheen, Lee
Strasberg, Lionel Stander, VALLI, O.J. SIMPSON

52.   THE SENTINEL. Universal, 1977 (c). *Michael Winner*. Sp: Jeffrey Konvitz
and Michael Winner, b/o novel by Jeffrey Konvitz. Cast: Chris Sarandon,
Cristina Raines, Burgess Meredith, Eli Wallach, Martin Balsam, Sylvia Miles,
Arthur Kennedy, John Carradine.

53. CITY ON FIRE (1979)
54. THE KIDNAPPING OF THE PRESIDENT (1980)
55. PRIEST OF LOVE 153 (1981)
56. REGINA (1982)   (over)

57. A.D. (1985) Ft
58. THE LONG HOT SUMMER (1985)
59 HAREM (1986)
60 MAGGIE (1986)

+ TV
5 EPISODES OF
KNOTS LANDING

INDEX

154

ABOUT THE AUTHOR
Judith M. Kass is the author of *Olivia de Havilland* and a study of Don Siegel in *The Hollywood Professionals*, vol. 4. She has written film criticism for *The Thousand Eyes* and *The Soho Weekly News* and is a contributor to *The Movie Buff's Book 2*. Ms. Kass has been the film programmer for The New York Cultural Center.

ABOUT THE EDITOR
Ted Sennett is the author of *Warner Brothers Presents*, a tribute to the great Warners films of the thirties and forties, and of *Lunatics and Lovers*, on the long-vanished but well-remembered "screwball" movie comedies of the past. He is also the editor of *The Movie Buff's Book*, *The Movie Buff's Book 2*, and *The Old-Time Radio Book*. He lives in New Jersey with his wife and three children.